D0385011

THE
NEW YORKER
BOOK OF GOLF CARTOONS

BLOOMBERG PRESS

PRINCETON

THE
NEW YORKER
BOOK OF GOLF CARTOONS

EDITED BY ROBERT MANKOFF

PUBLISHED BY BLOOMBERG PRESS

Copyright © 2002 by The New Yorker Magazine, Inc.

All art is protected by registrations and renewals duly filed with the Register of Copyrights, Library of Congress, by The New Yorker Magazine, Inc.

The magazine's name and logo are protected by registrations duly filed with the Patent and Trademark Office, and in trademark registries abroad.

All rights reserved. Protected under the Berne Convention. Printed in the United States of America. No part of this book may be reproduced, stored in a retrieval system, or transmitted, in any form or by any means, electronic, mechanical, photocopying, recording, or otherwise, without the prior written permission of CARTOONBANK.COM except in the case of brief quotations embodied in critical articles and reviews. For information, please write: Permissions Department, Bloomberg Press, 100 Business Park Drive, P.O. Box 888, Princeton, NJ 08542-0888 U.S.A.

To purchase framed prints of cartoons or to license cartoons for use in periodicals, Web sites, or other media, please contact CARTOONBANK.COM, a New Yorker Magazine company, at 145 Palisade Street, Suite 373, Dobbs Ferry, NY 10522, Tel: 800-897-TOON, or (914) 478-5527, Fax: (914) 478-5604, e-mail: toon@cartoonbank.com, Web: www.cartoonbank.com.

Books are available for bulk purchases at special discounts. Special editions or book excerpts can also be created to specifications. For information, please write: Special Markets Department, Bloomberg Press.

BLOOMBERG, THE BLOOMBERG, BLOOMBERG NEWS, BLOOMBERG FINANCIAL MARKETS, and BLOOMBERG PRESS are trademarks and service marks of Bloomberg L.P. All rights reserved.

First edition published 2002
1 3 5 7 9 10 8 6 4 2

Library of Congress Cataloging-in-Publication Data

The New Yorker book of golf cartoons / edited by Robert Mankoff.
    p. cm.
    Includes index.
    ISBN 1-57660-119-6 (alk. paper)
    1. Golf--Caricatures and cartoons. 2. American wit and humor, Pictorial. 3. New Yorker (New York, N.Y. : 1925) I. Title: Book of golf cartoons, II. Mankoff, Robert. III. New Yorker (New York, N.Y. : 1925)

NC1428 .N47 2002
741.5'973--dc21   2002016333

Book design by LAURIE LOHNE / Design It Communications

THE
NEW YORKER
BOOK OF GOLF CARTOONS

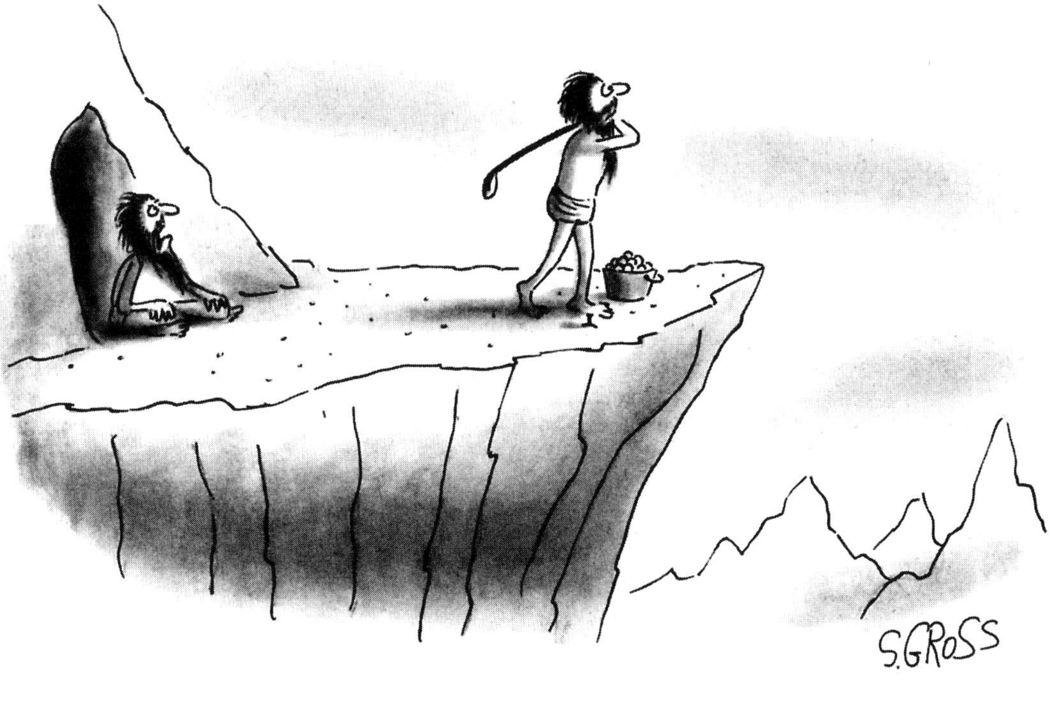
S.GROSS

"If you're so enlightened, how come you can't lick that slice?"

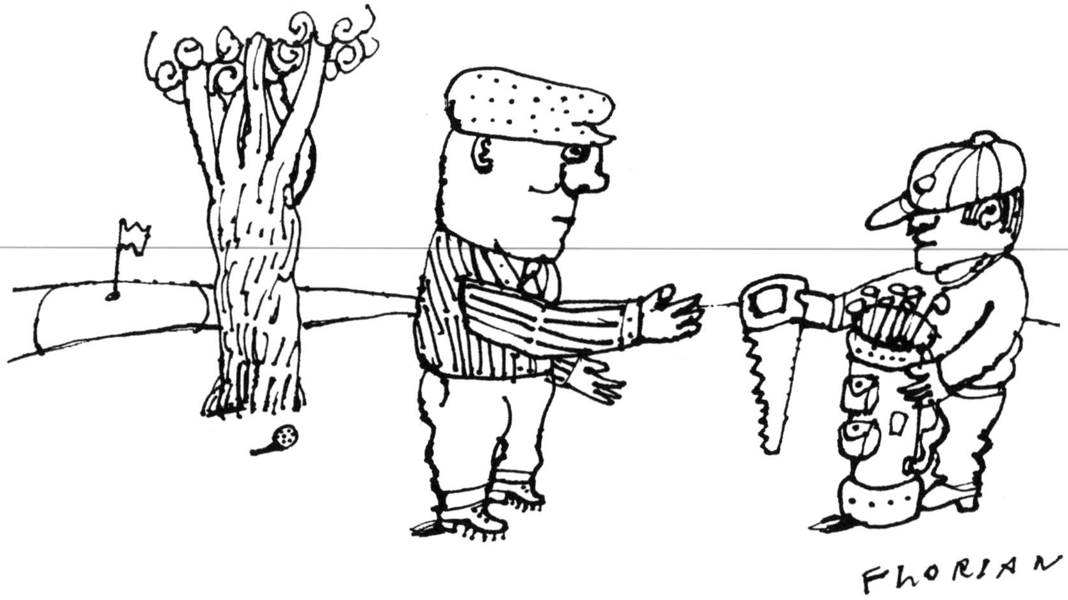
FLORIAN

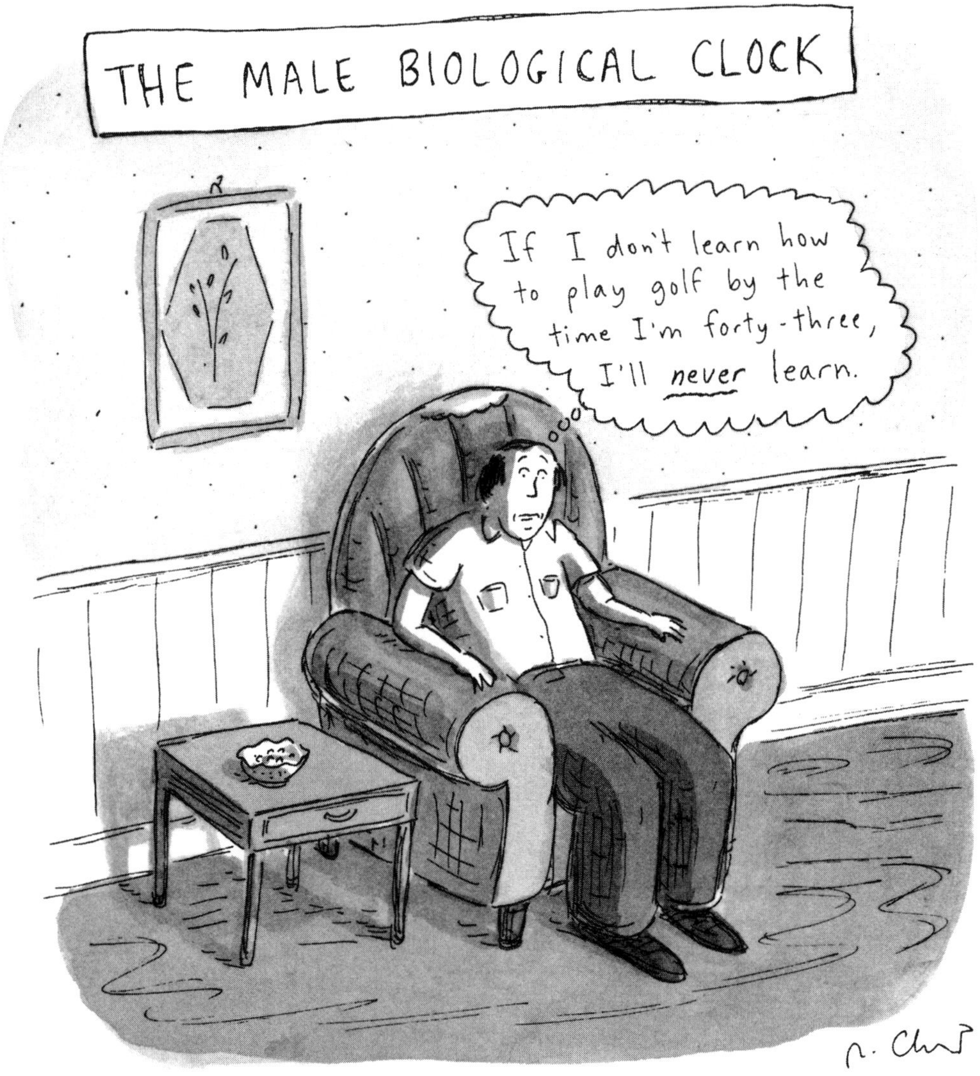
THE MALE BIOLOGICAL CLOCK
If I don't learn how to play golf by the time I'm forty-three, I'll never learn.

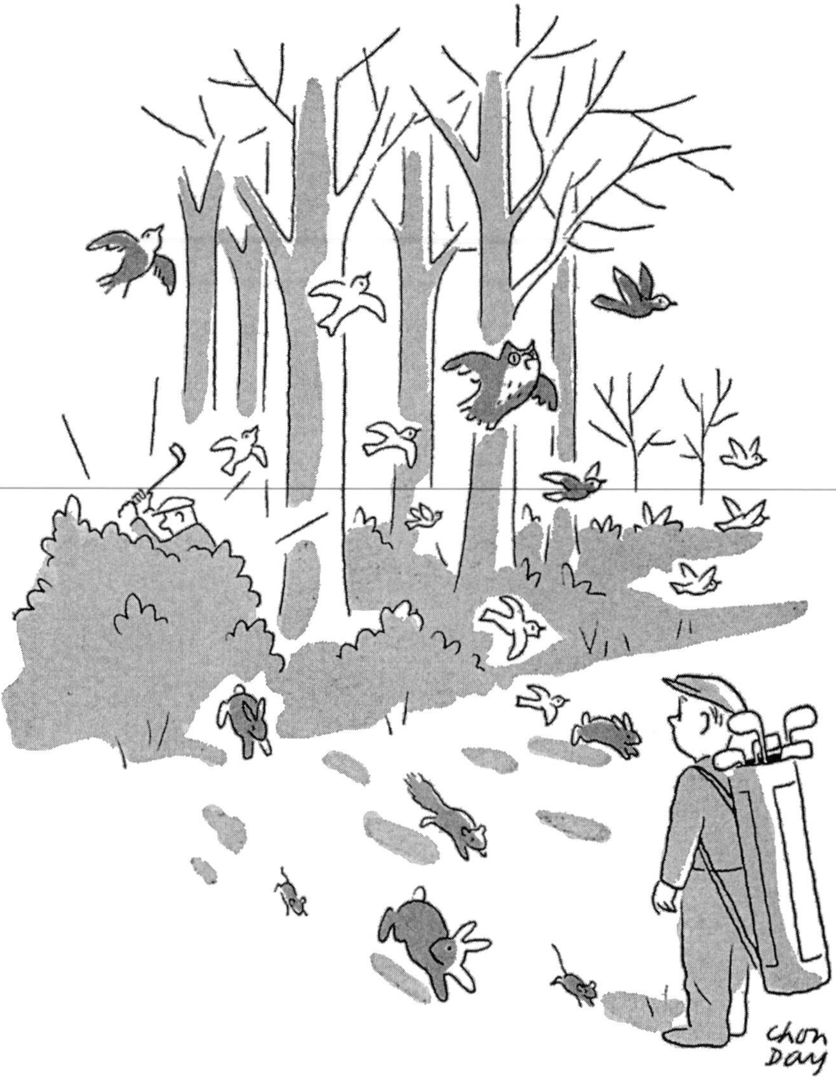

CHON DAY

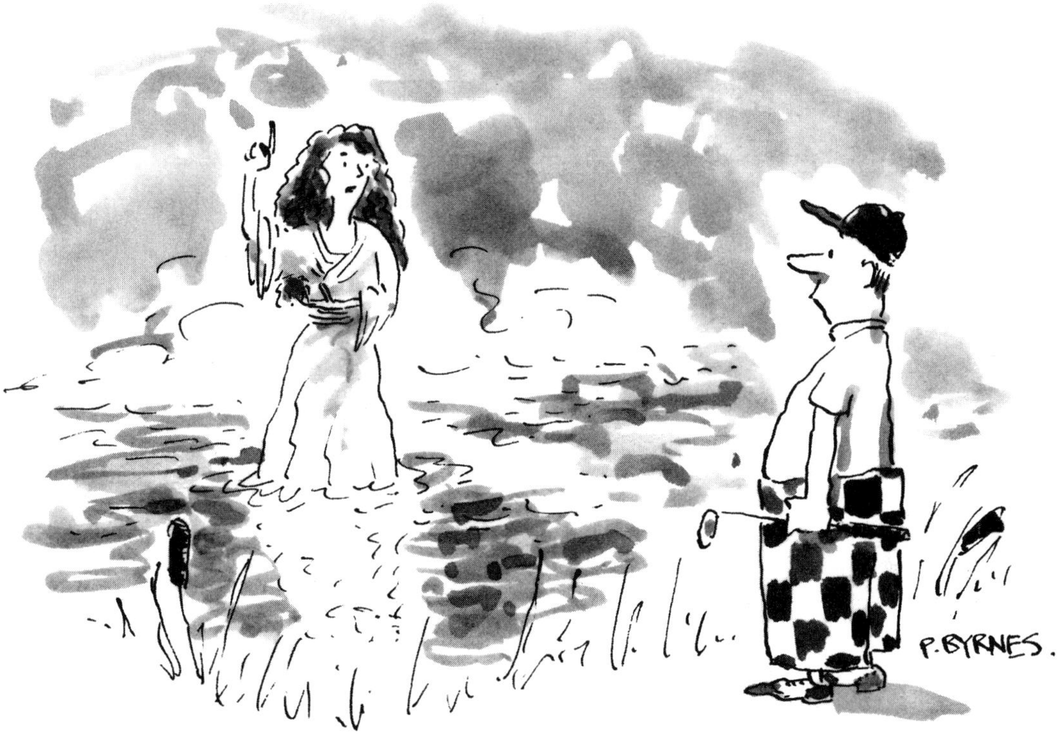
P. BYRNES.

"I am the Lady of the Lake, and because thou hast defiled my crystal waters I must hence smite thee. That or penalize thee a stroke. Your call."

"Gotta run, sweetheart. By the way, that was one fabulous job you did raising the children."

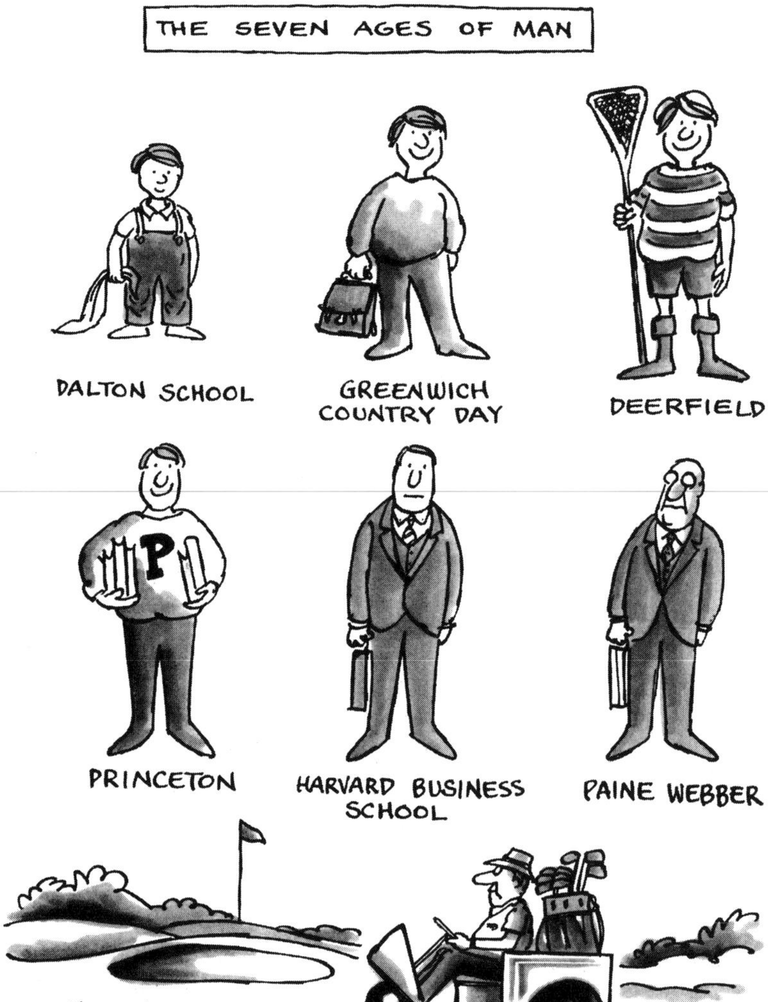
THE SEVEN AGES OF MAN
DALTON SCHOOL
GREENWICH COUNTRY DAY
DEERFIELD
PRINCETON
HARVARD BUSINESS SCHOOL
PAINE WEBBER
HILTON HEAD

"Bankruptcy doesn't seem to have hurt your putting eye a bit, Pete."

1

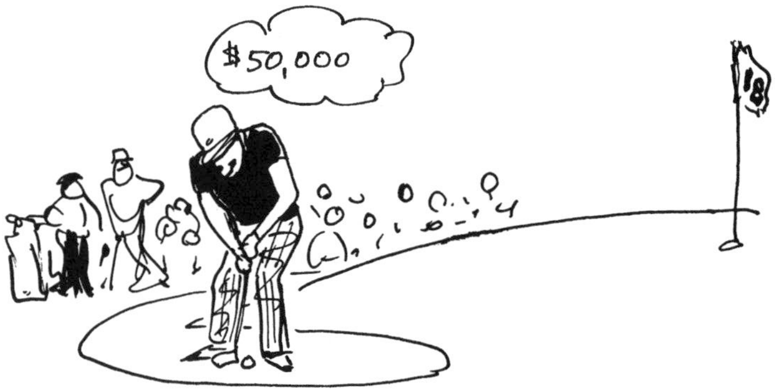
$50,000

3

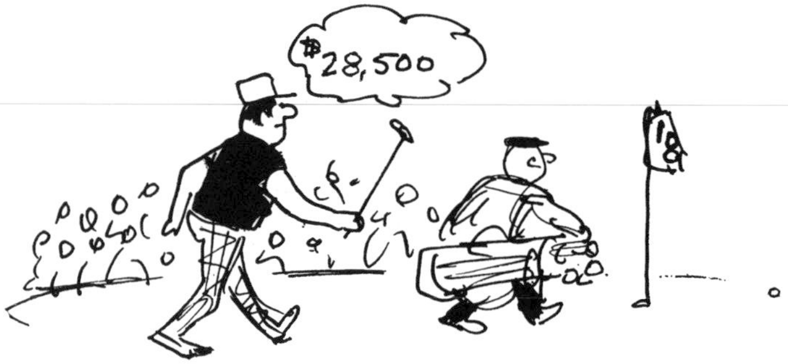
$28,500

5

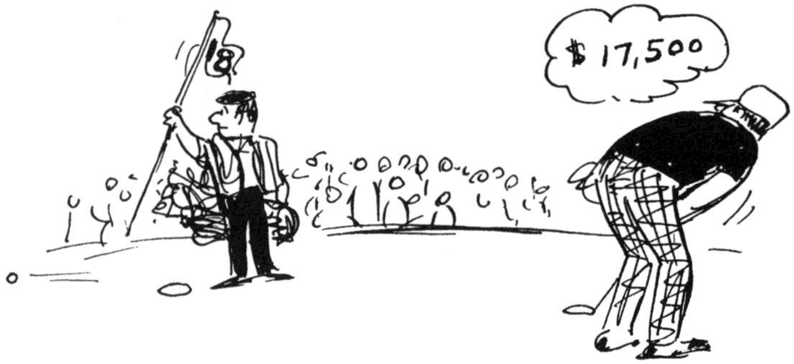
$17,500

2

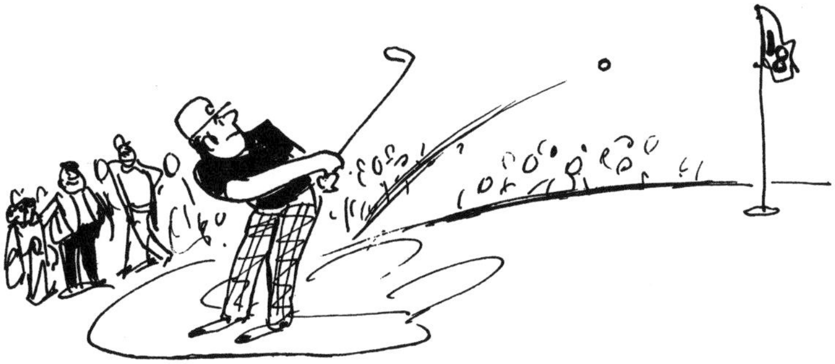
18

4

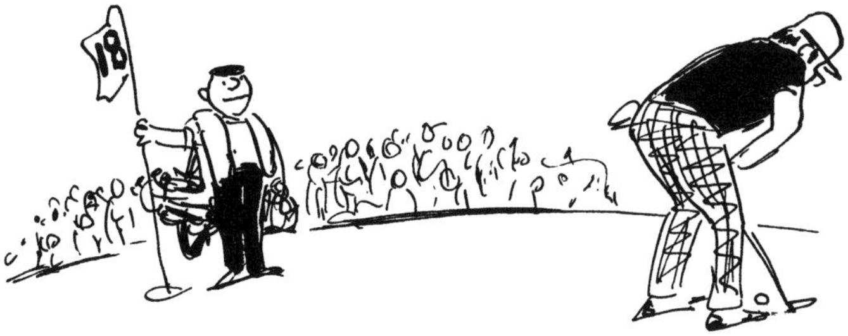
18

6

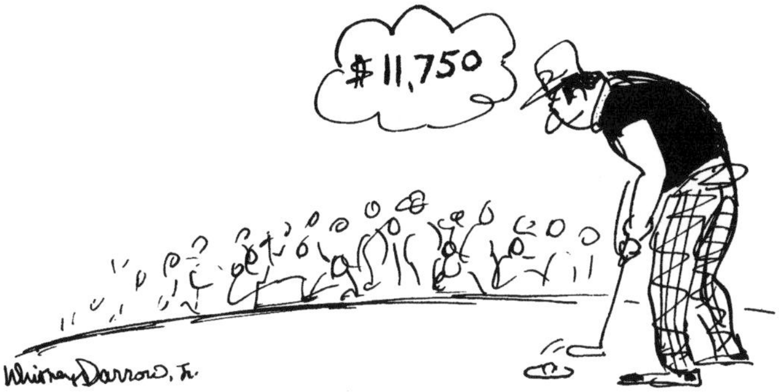
$11,750
Whitney Darrow, Jr.

"Oh, for goodness' sake, forget it, Beasley. Play another one."

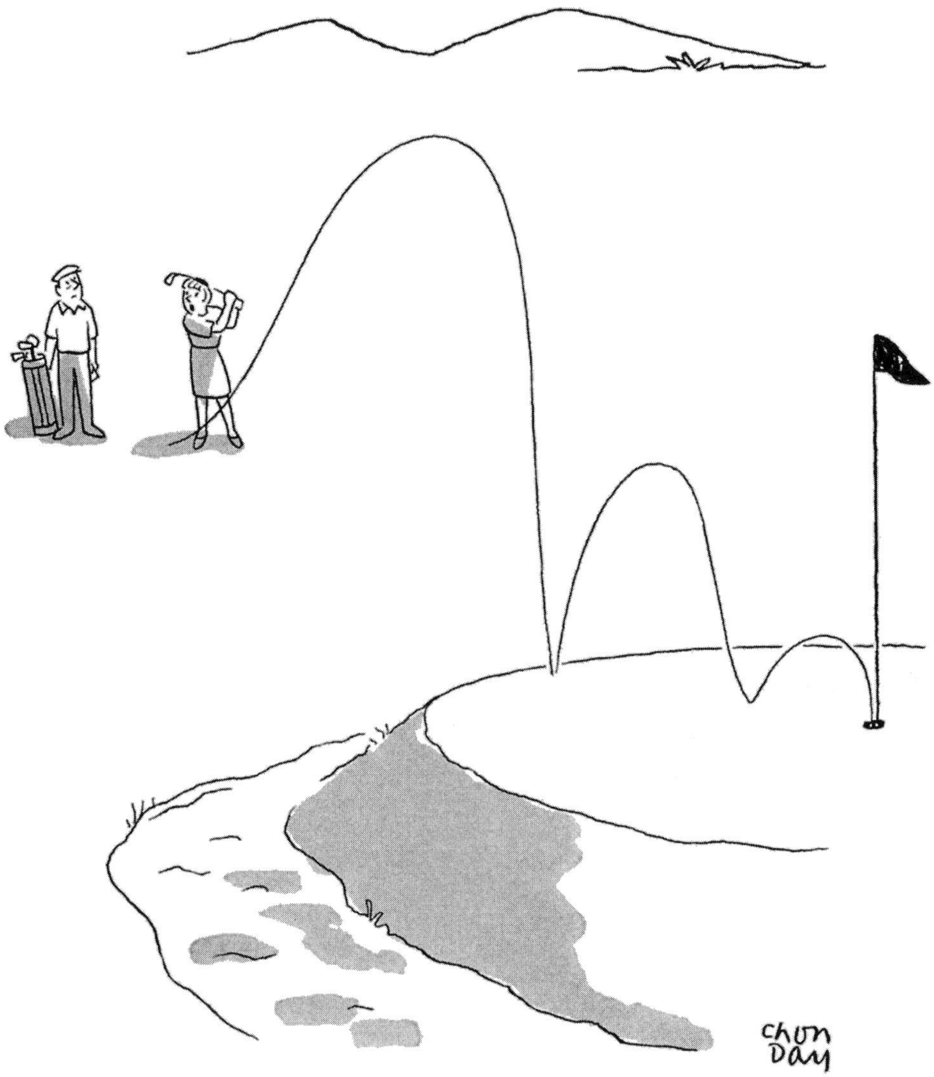
CHON DAY

"Like so?"

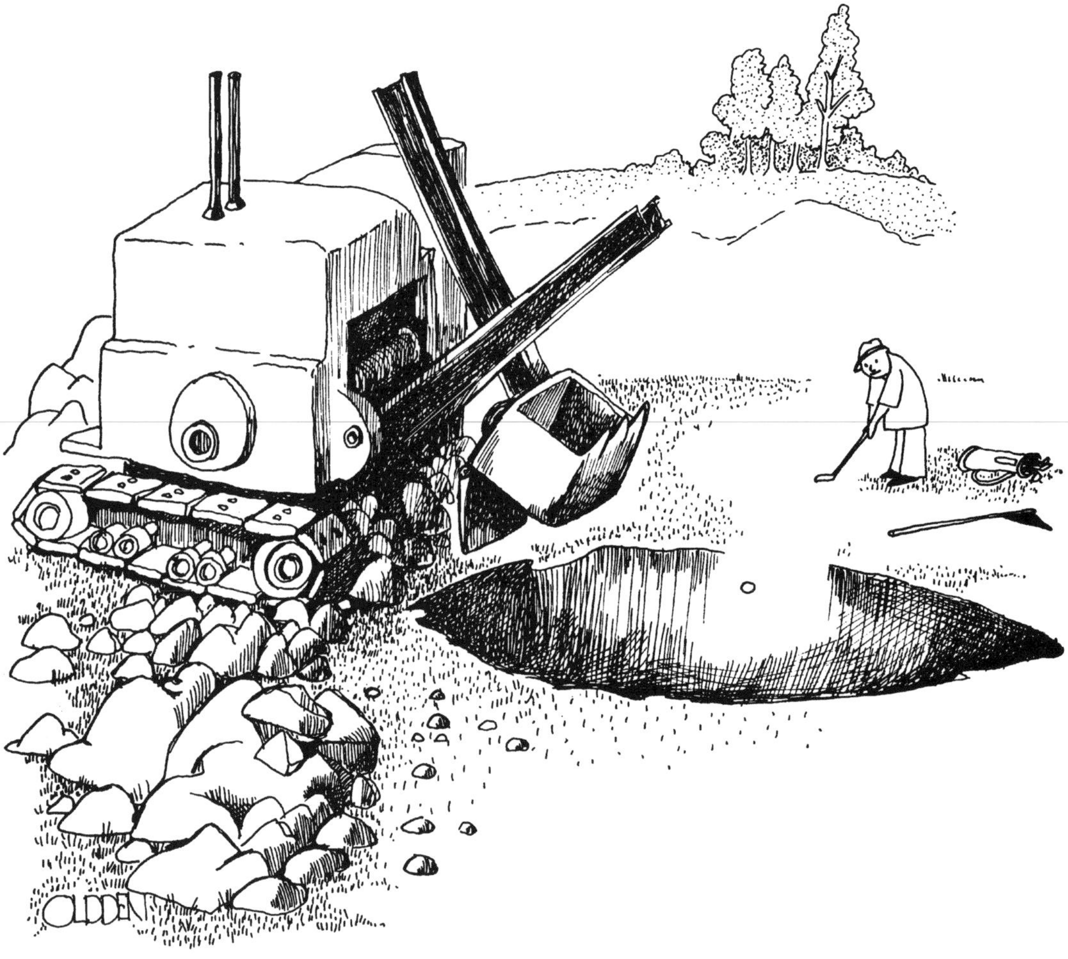
OLDDEN

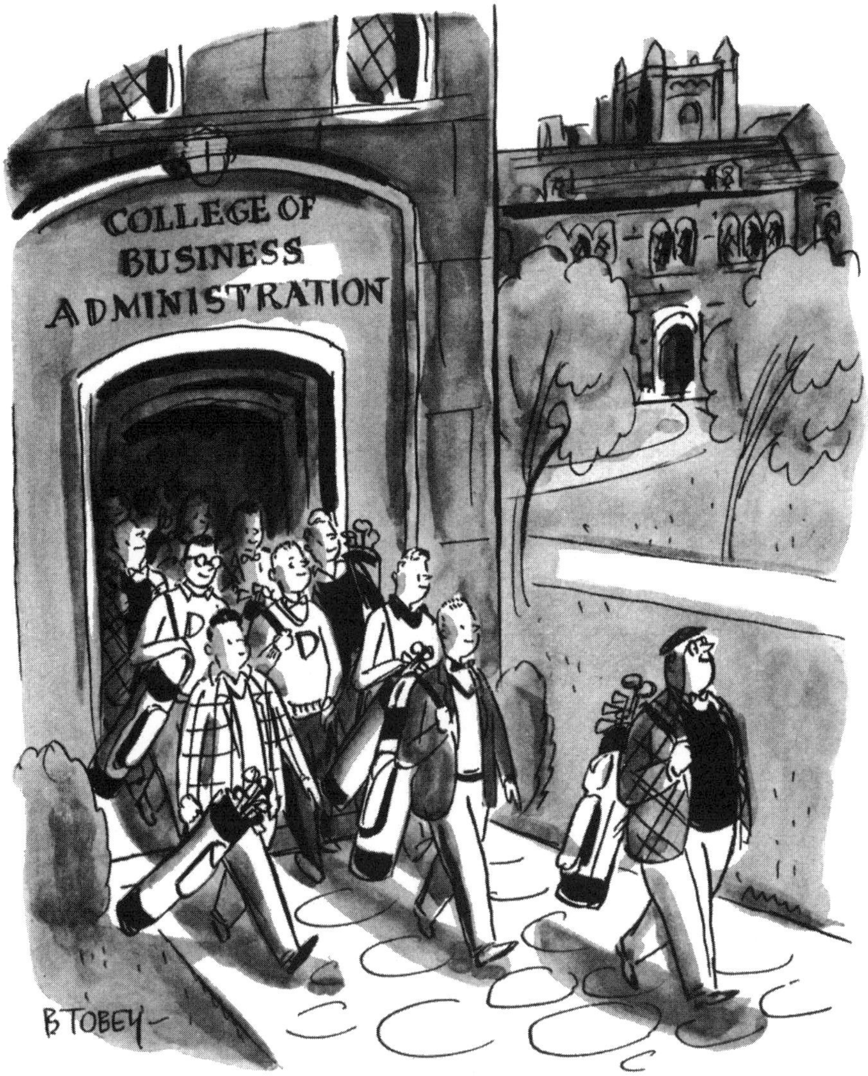
COLLEGE OF
BUSINESS
ADMINISTRATION
B TOBEY

"You know something, Jeff?   There *is* one place we haven't looked."

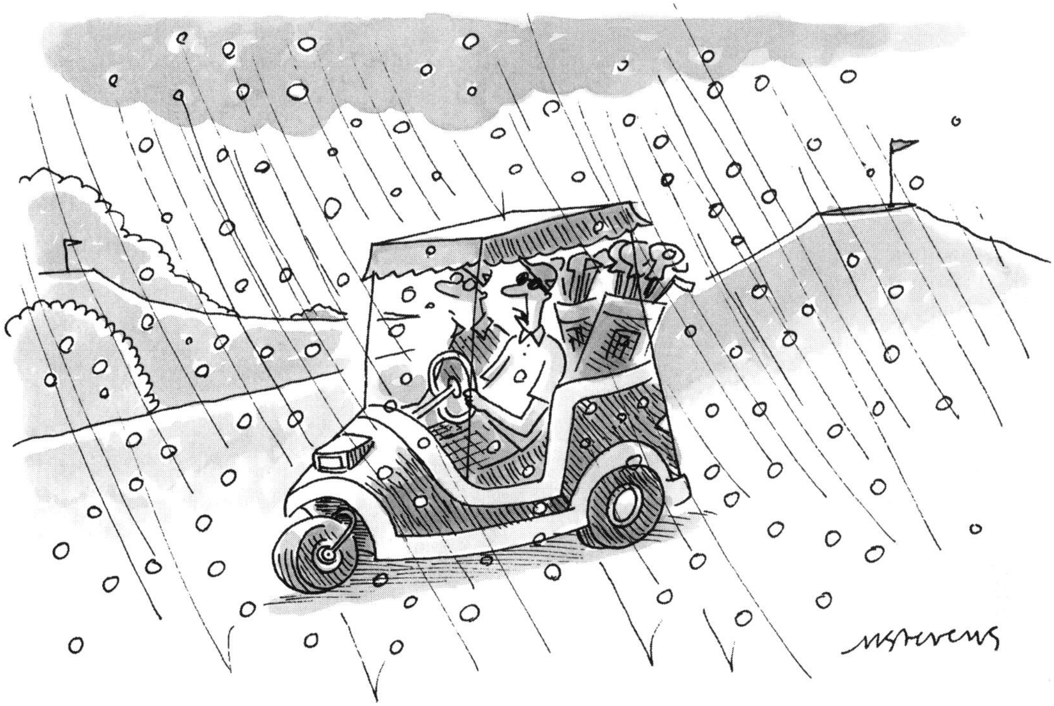
MSTEVENS

"Oh, no! Golf ball–sized hail!"

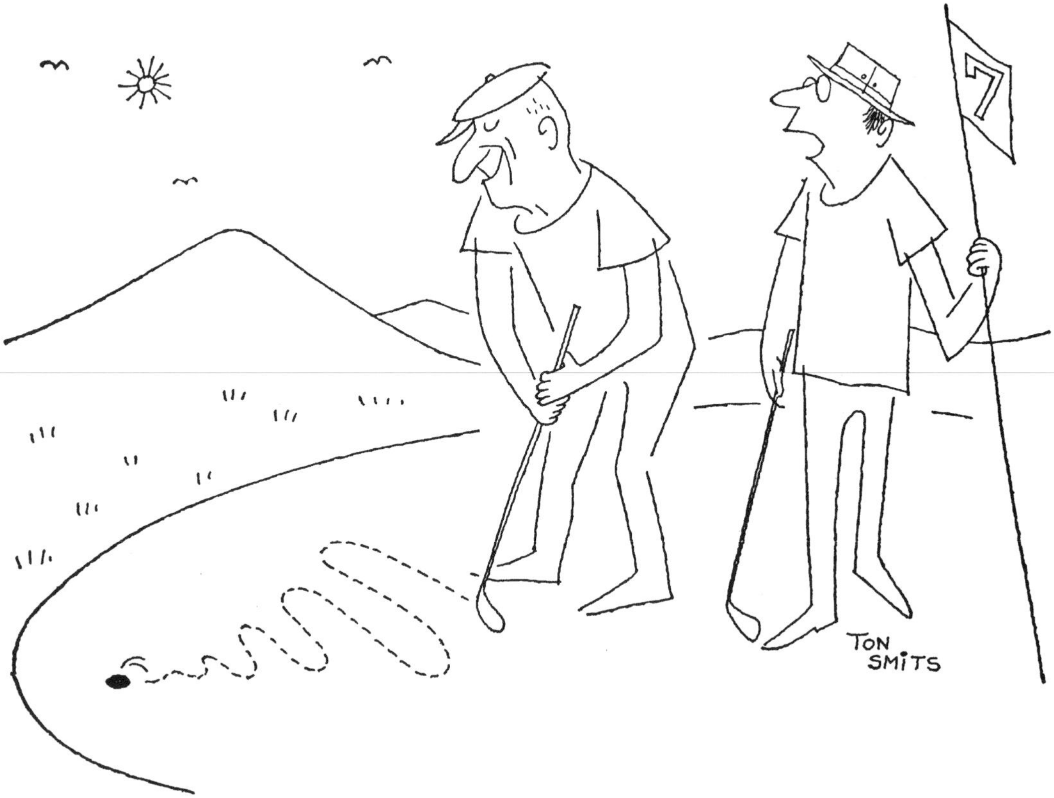
7
TON SMITS

"You've been drinking."

"It's the old story. East Hampton isn't big enough for both of them."

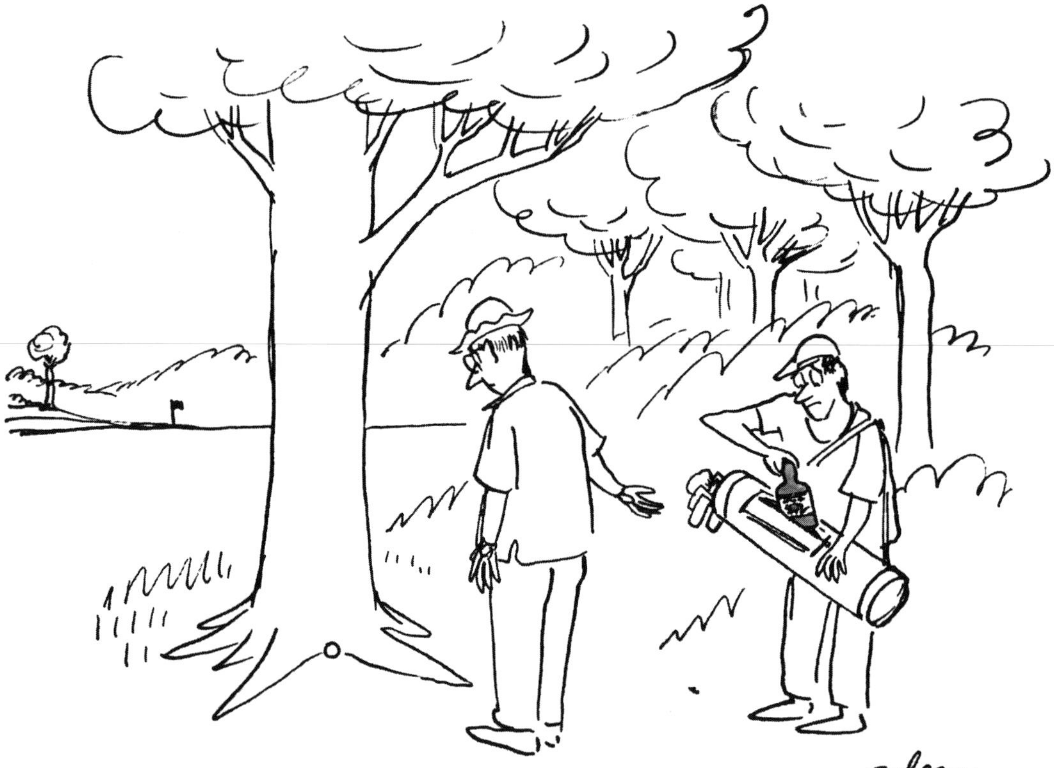
cobean

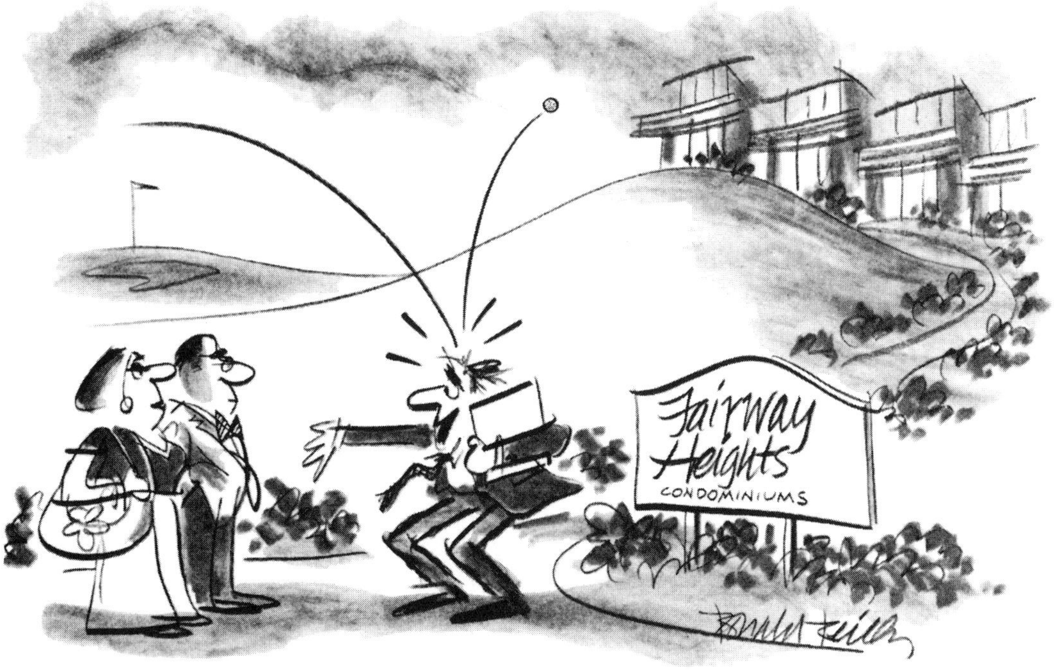

Fairway
Heights
CONDOMINIUMS

"...and, of course, the fairways are—eee-yi!—right at your doorstep."

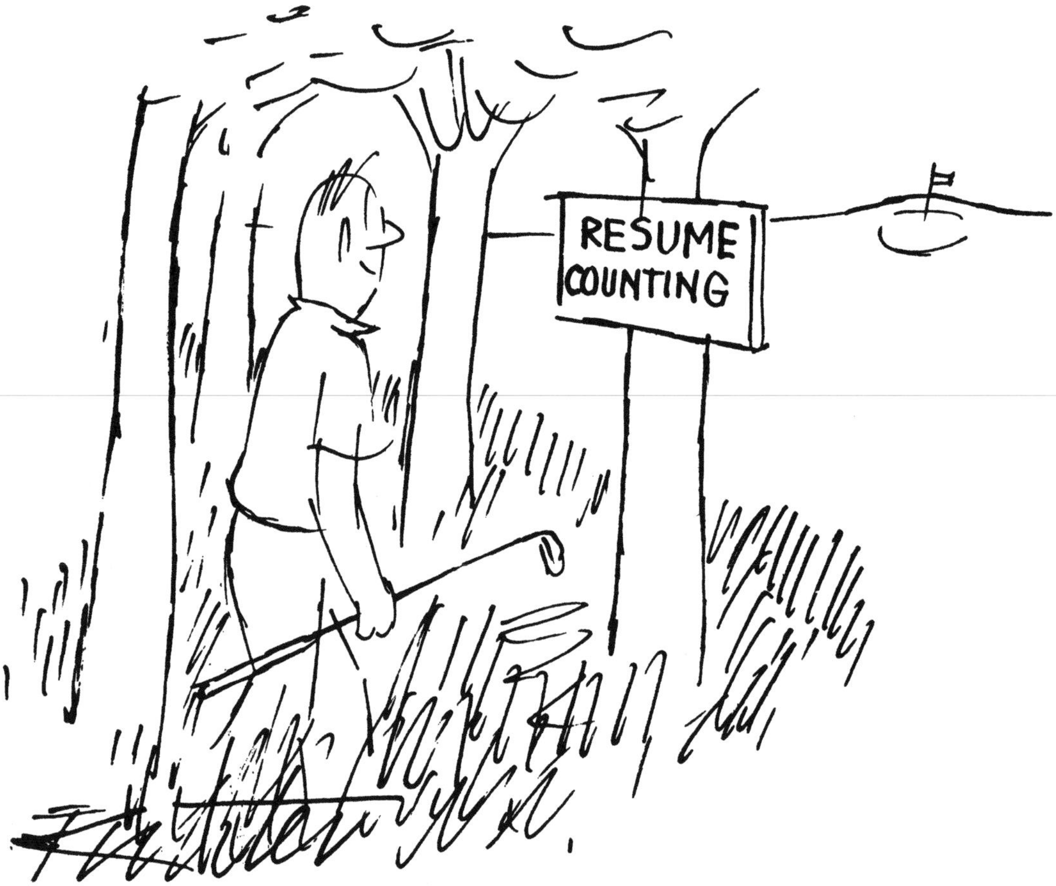
RESUME
COUNTING

"He's sure taking long enough. Probably figuring his new bracket if he sinks it."

"*Use a five iron!*"

*"I'm perfectly furious! It would have gone another
fifty yards if he hadn't got in the way."*

1

2

3

4

5

6

7

8

Robt Day

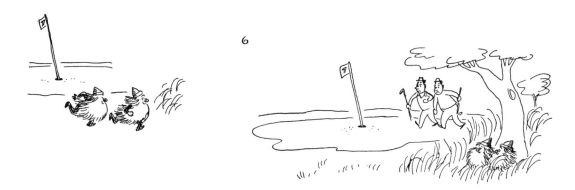

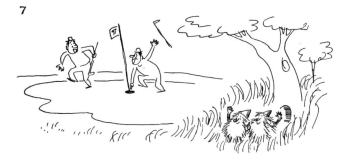

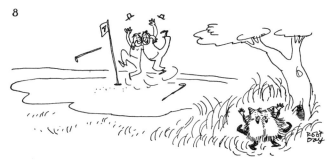

"I wish I could stay out of the rough
long enough to find out if I'm any good at this game."

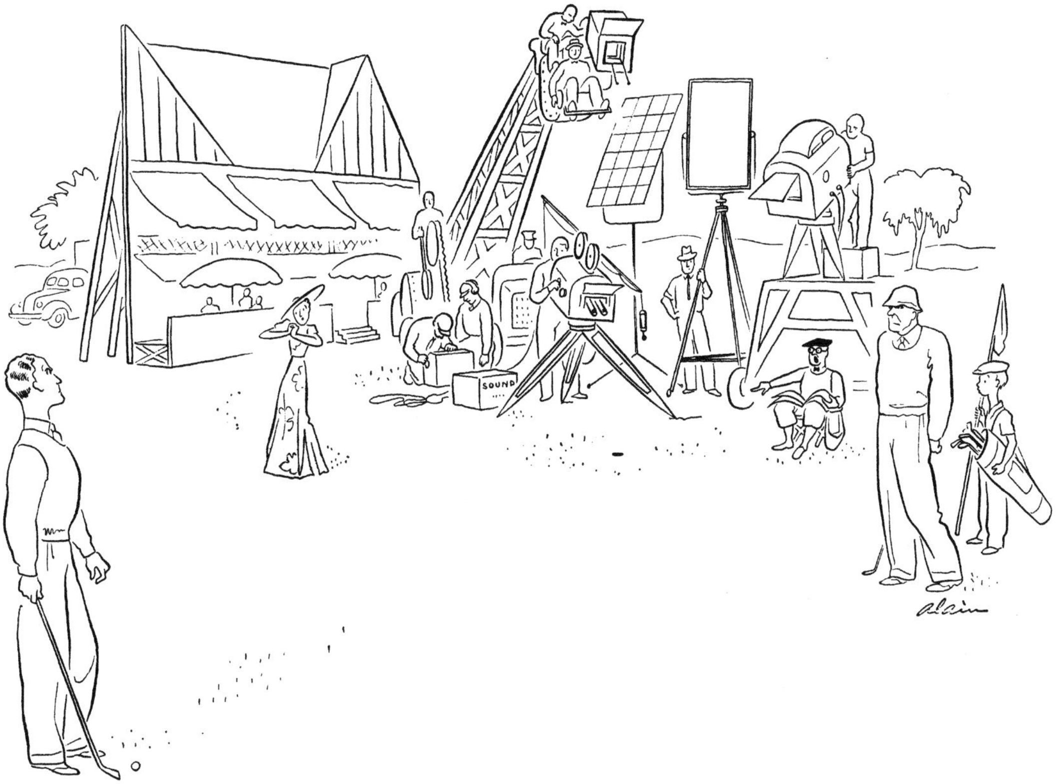
SOUND

"Understand now? The ball must roll to the edge of the cup, waver, and drop in."

"*There now, wouldn't it have been silly of me to concede that putt?*"

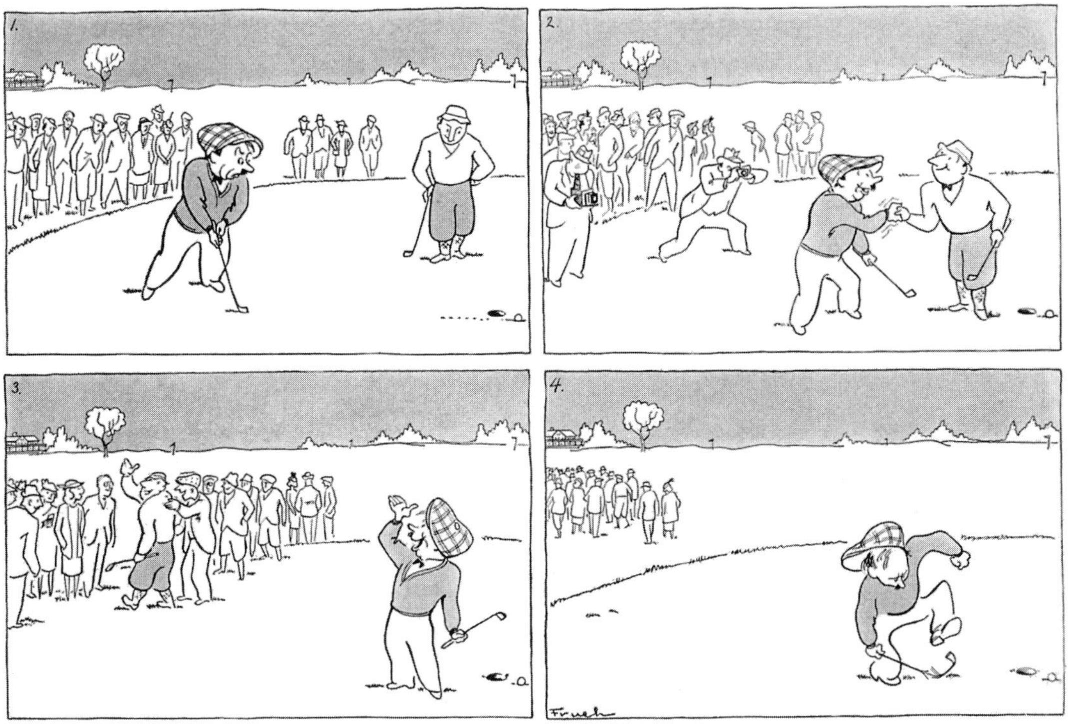
1.
2.
3.
4.
Frueh

"*Let me think. Where would I go*
if I were a golf ball?"

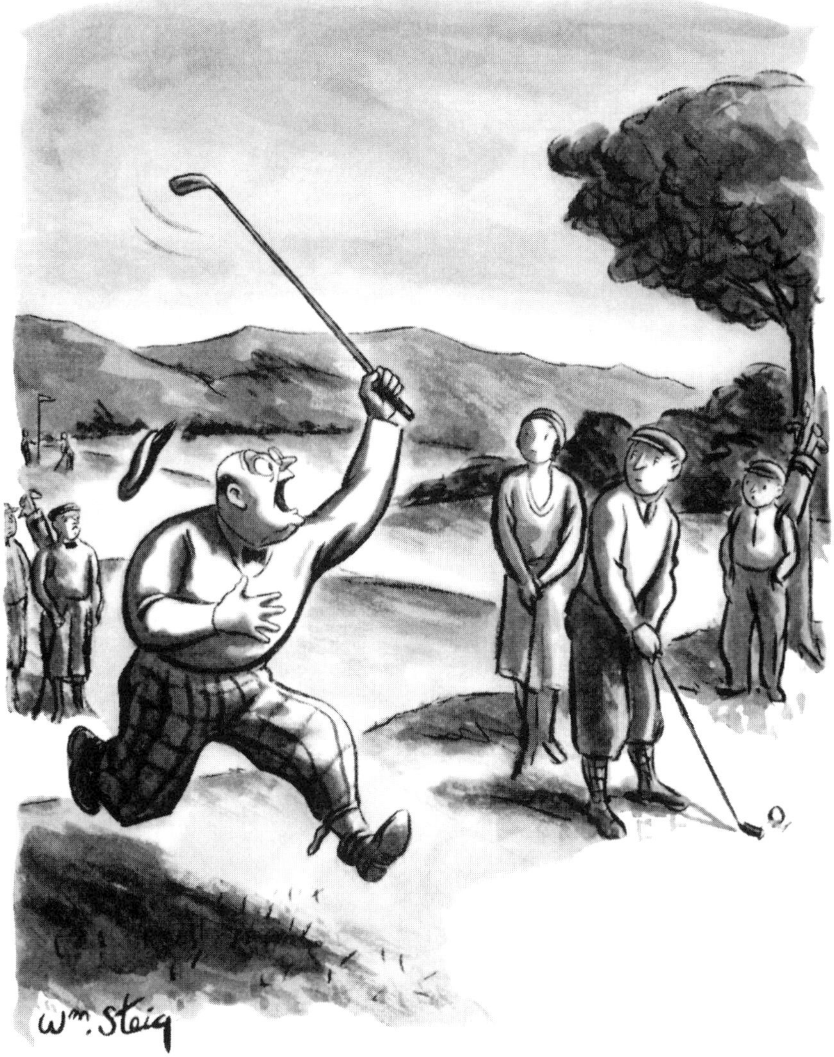
Wm. Steig

"A hole in one! Me! I'm going cra-zy!"

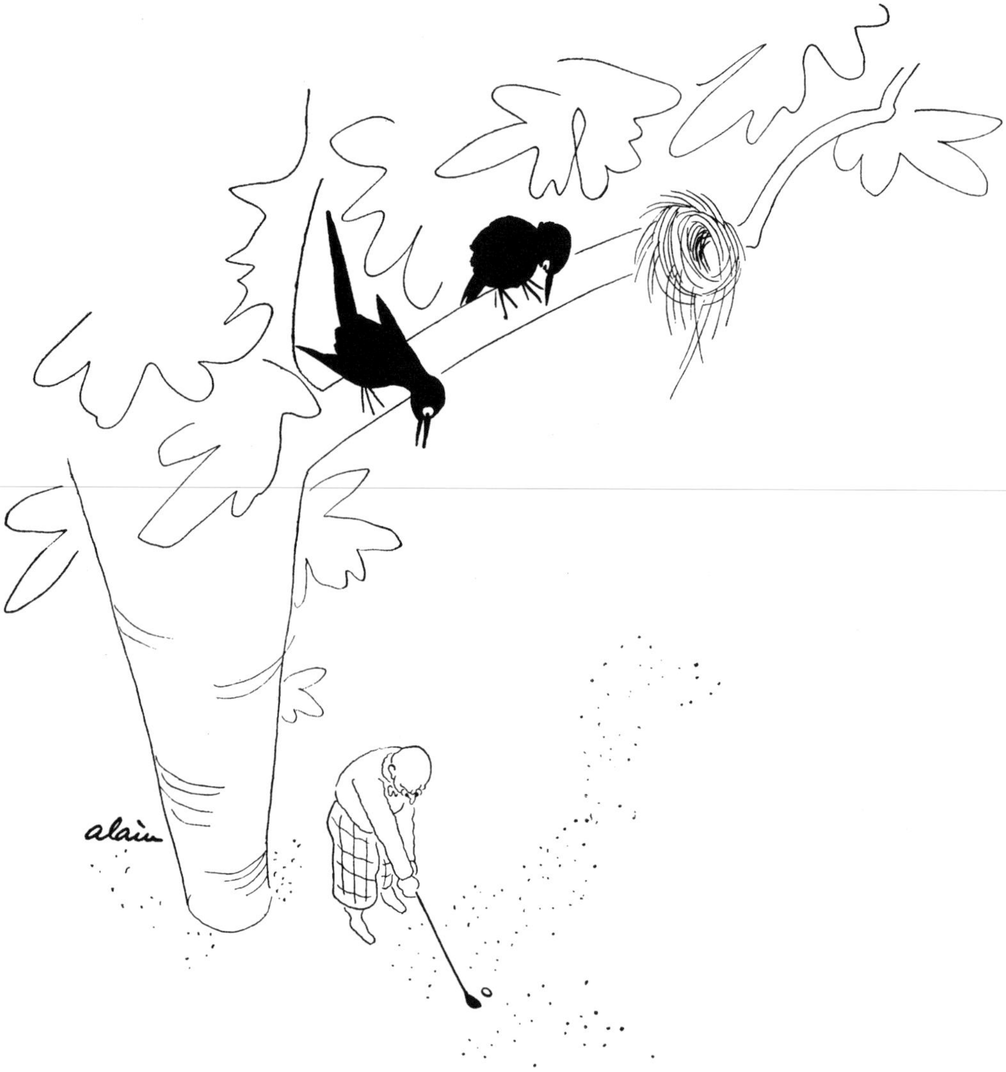
alain

"Well, there goes Junior."

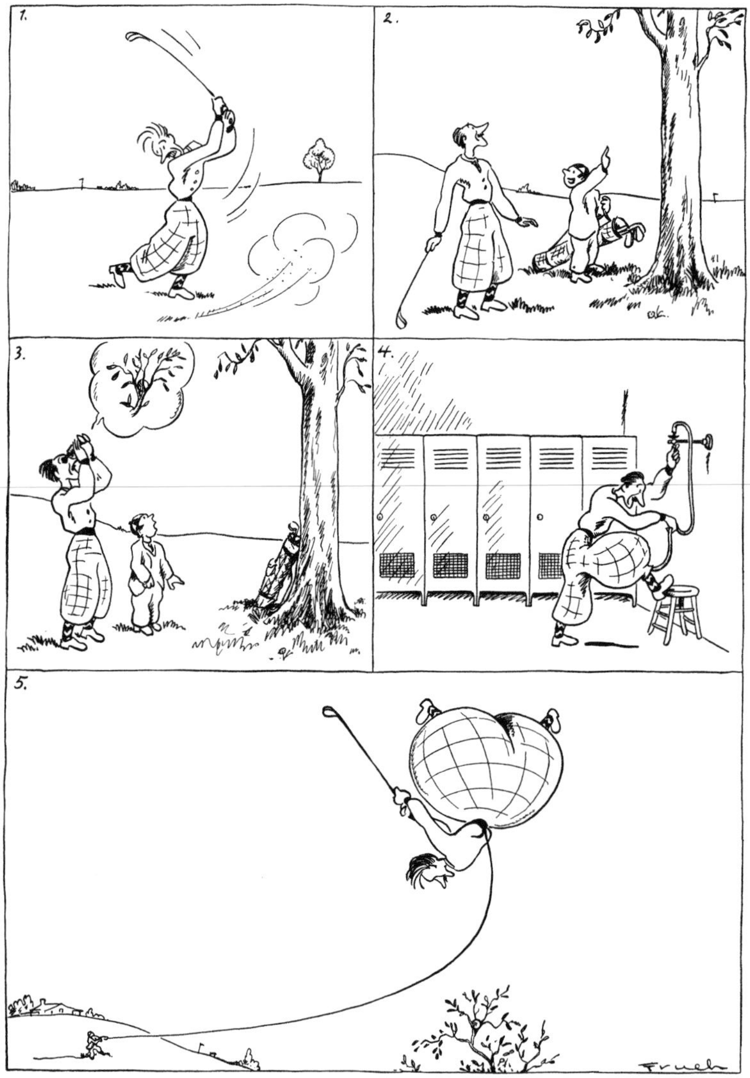
1.
2.
3.
4.
5.
Frueh

"*Wilson always was a poor loser.*"

*"Would you mind picking
me up, Bill? Agnes is using the car after all."*

"It's Daddy, Mom. And he's _smiling!_"

"Here's one you'll understand."

"It's a poor workman, Malcolm, who blames his tools."

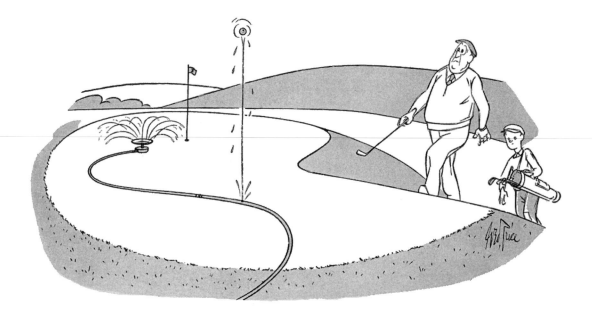

"*Will you stop saying it's all a part of the game? It's <u>not</u> part of the game.*"

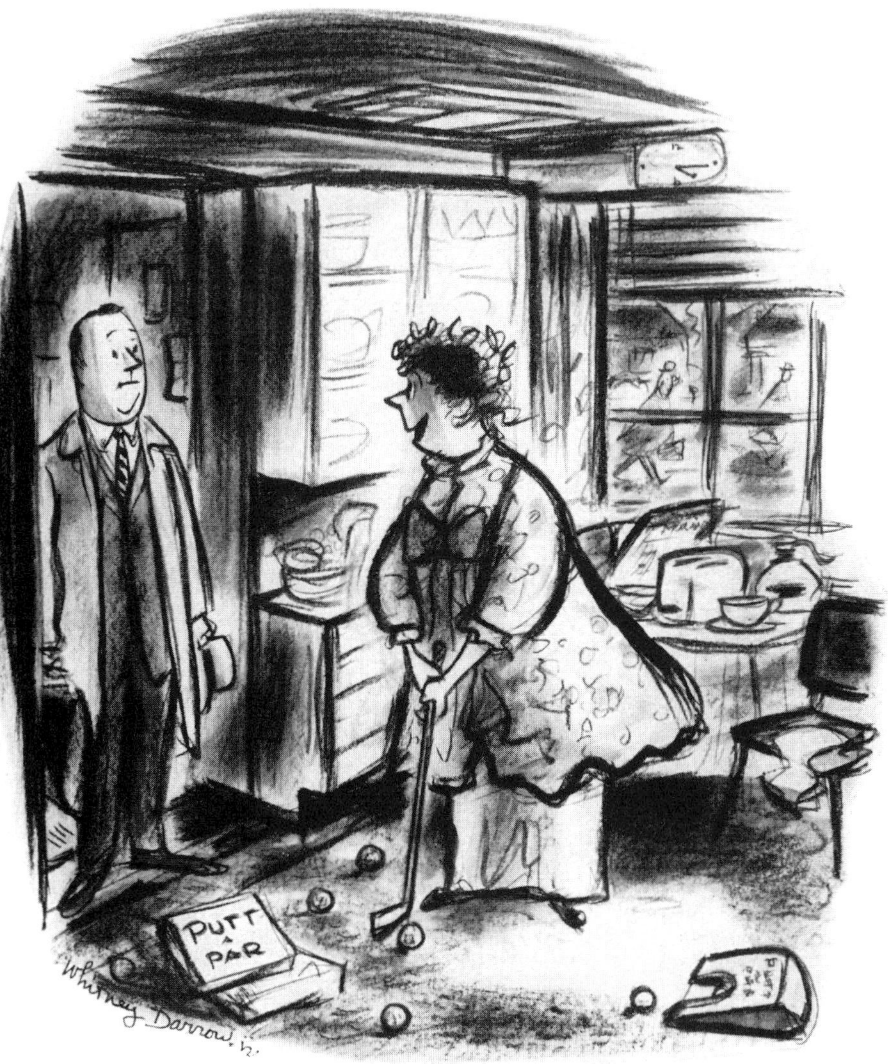
PUTT
A
PAR
Whitney Darrow, Jr.

"Darling, golf is fun."

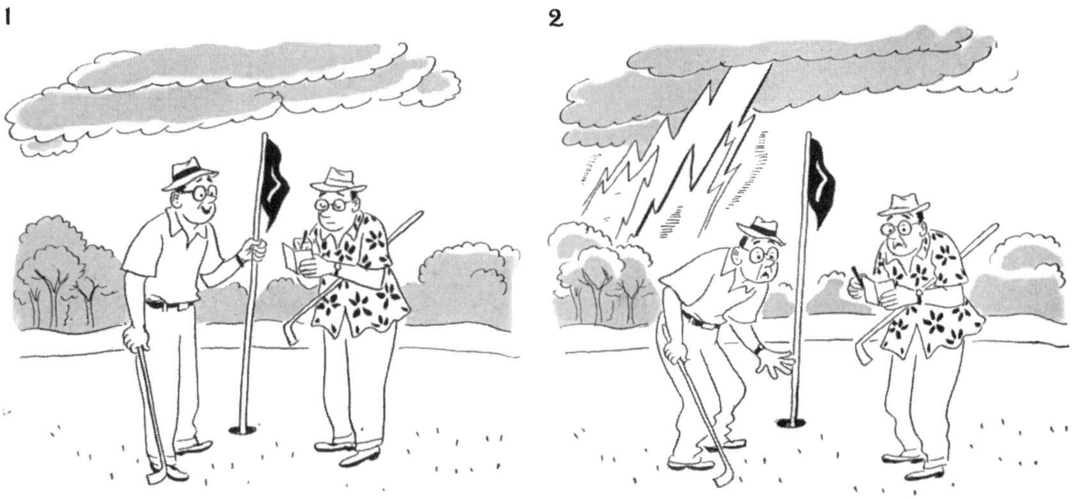
1
2

"A four for me."

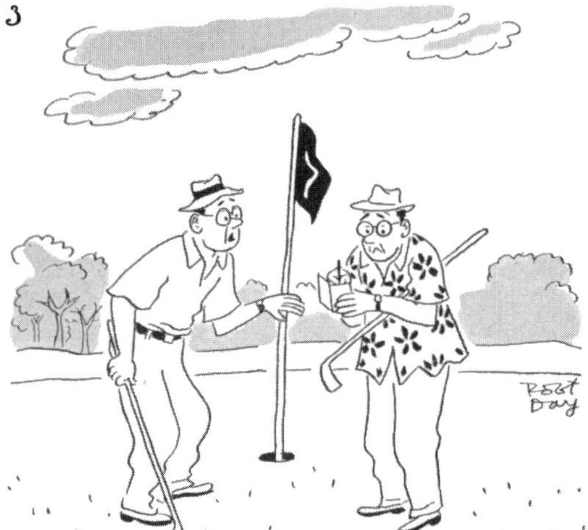
3
Robt Day

"I mean six."

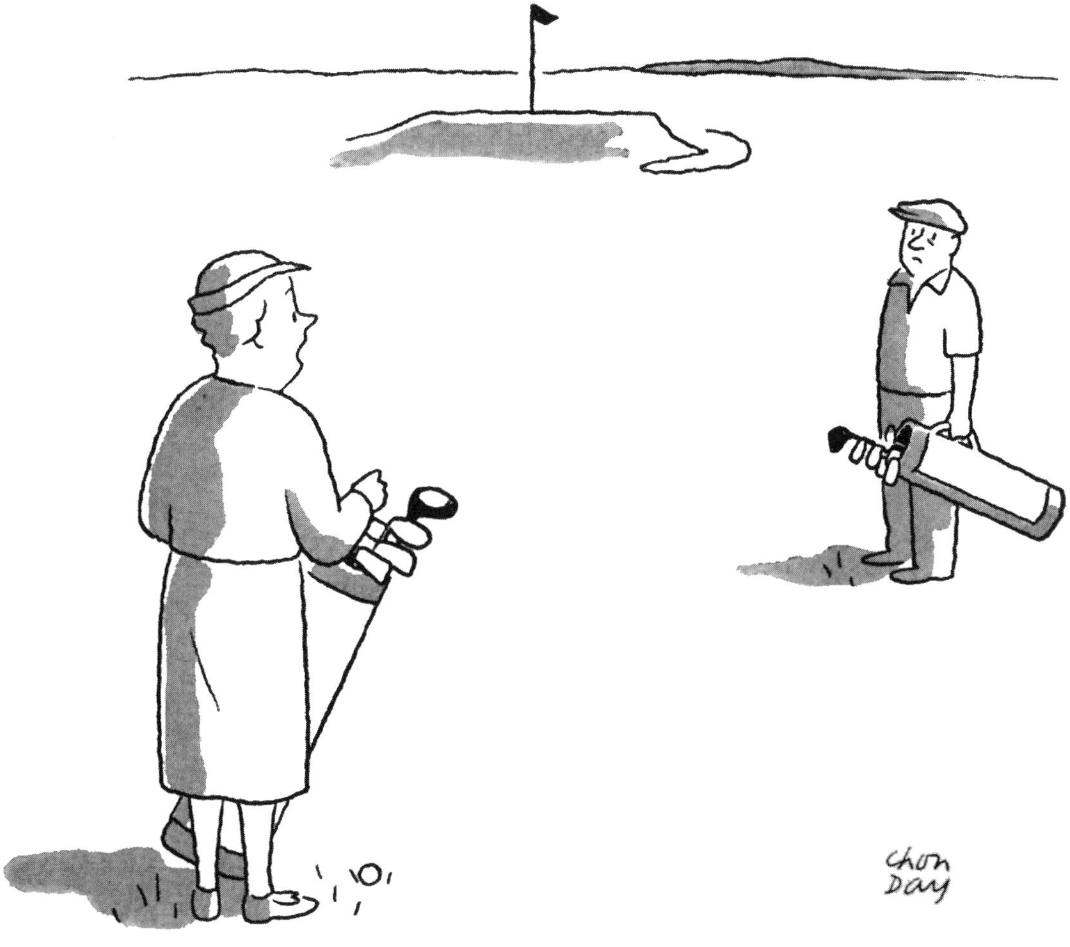
Chon
Day

"Is that the big one with the knob, or one of the little scoops?"

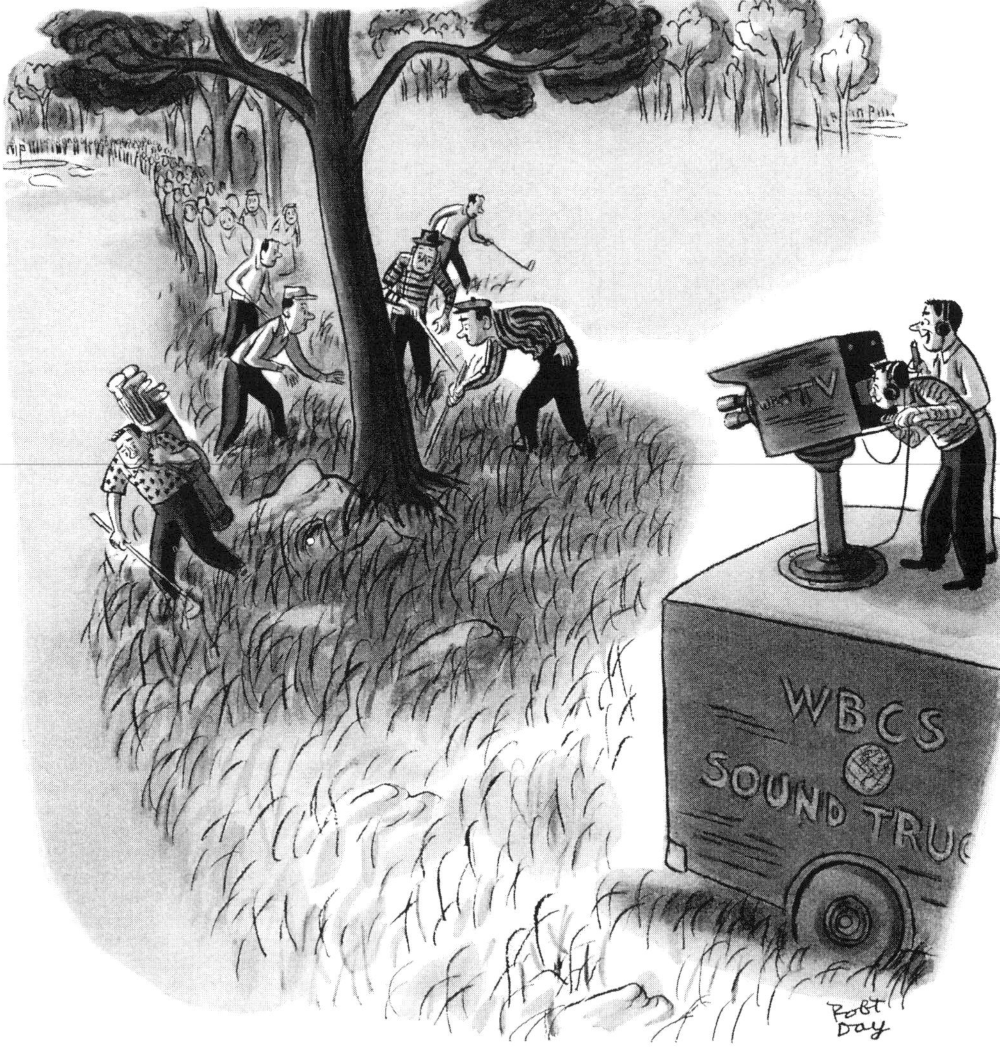
WBCS
SOUND TRUC

"See it, folks, just to the left of that tree? All right, you people at home know where it is. Now let's see how long it takes them to find it."

"I did not say it wasn't a super-shot. I merely said that I, personally, was not electrified."

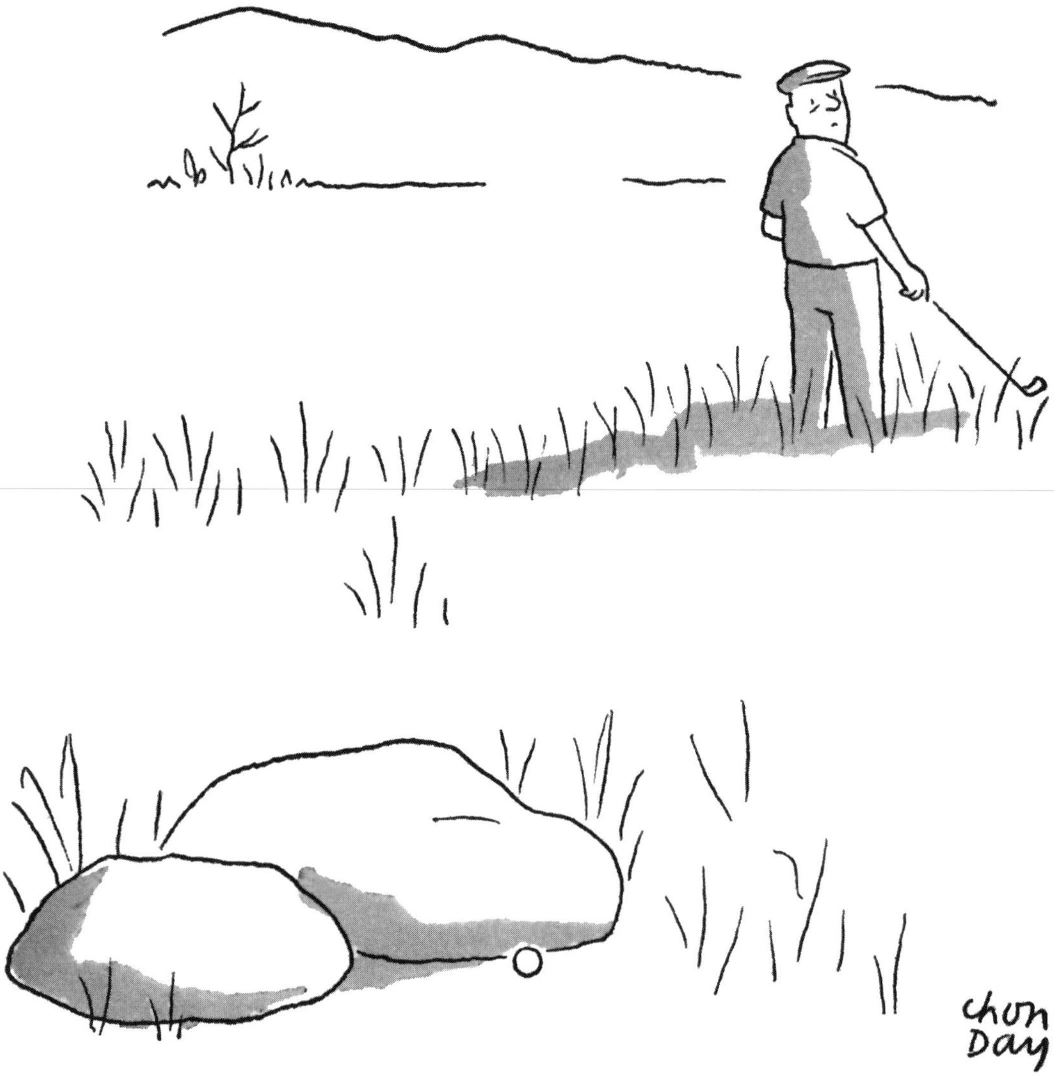
chon
Day

"Here I am."

"You're going to shoot a hundred and fourteen, dear."

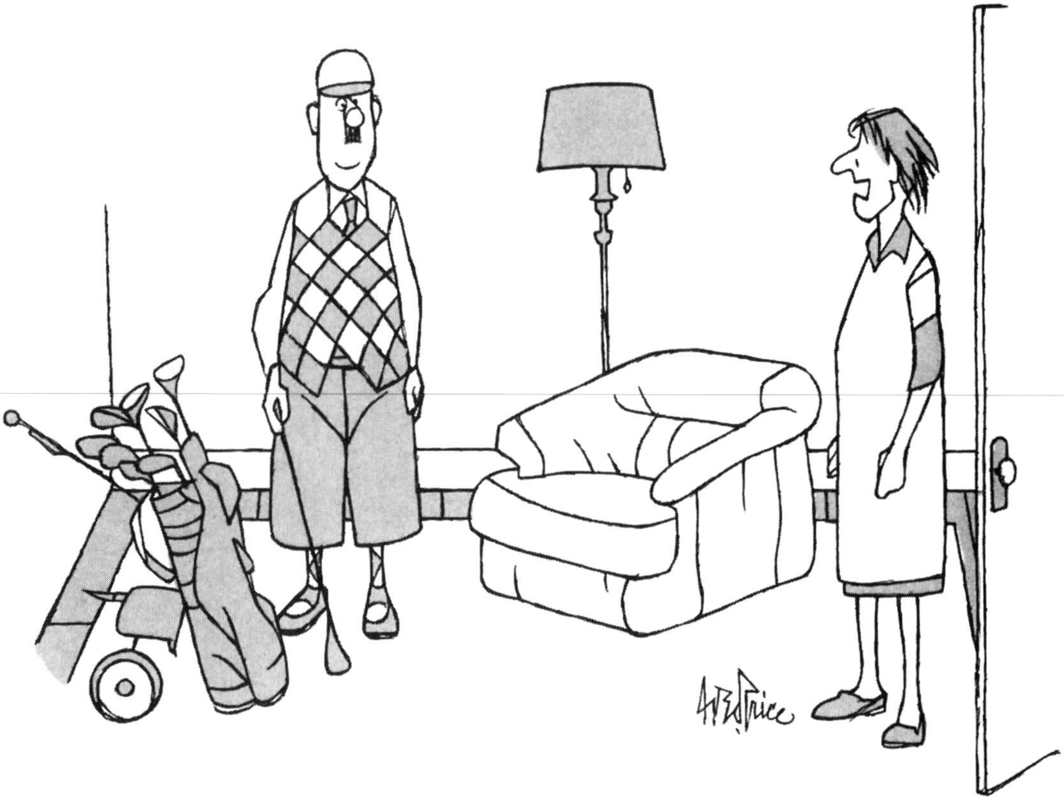

George Price

"All right, they're coming back. Couldn't you have waited until they got here?"

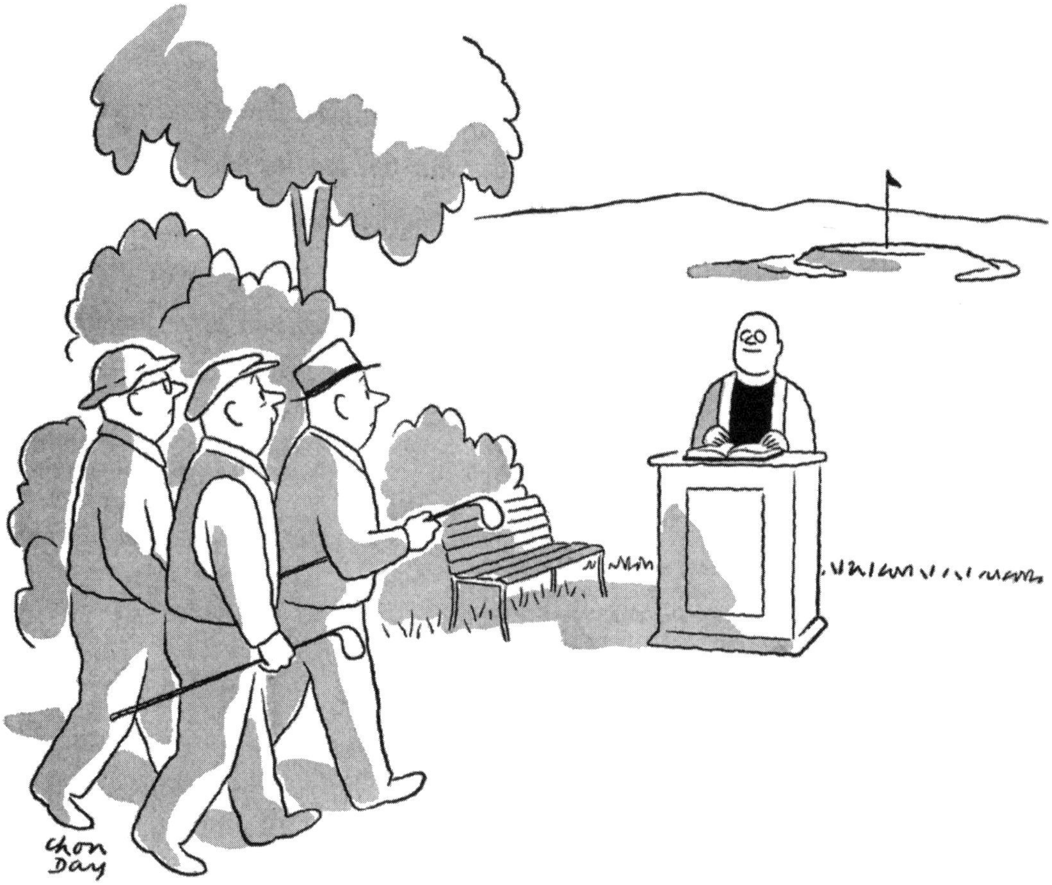
Chon Day

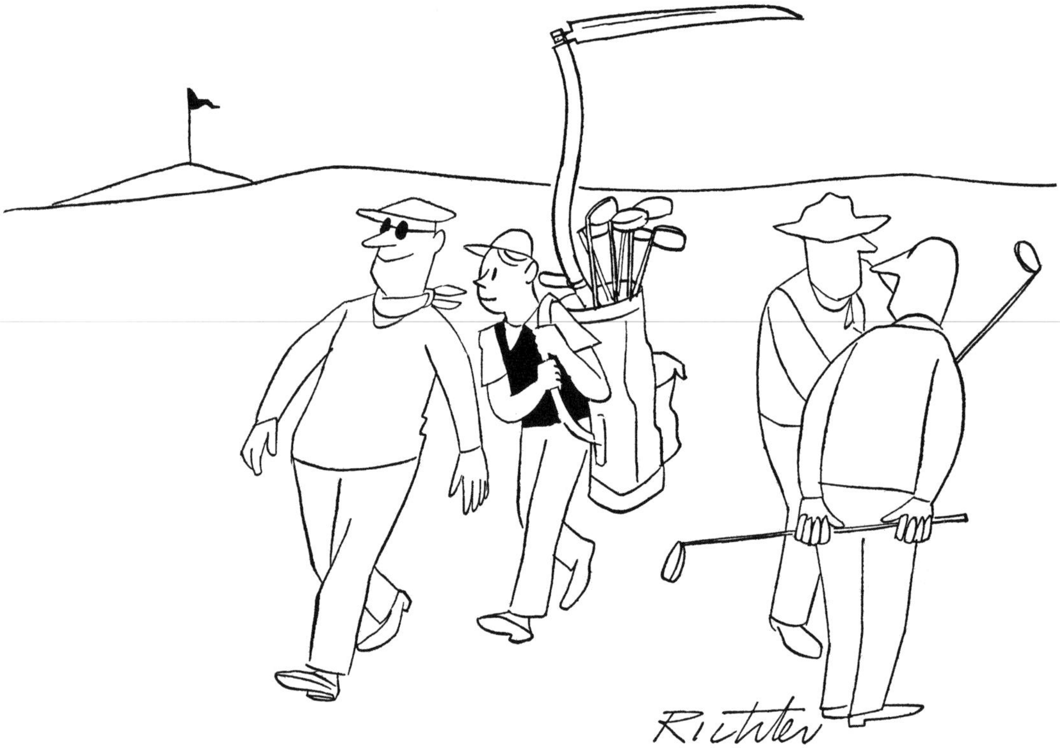
Richter

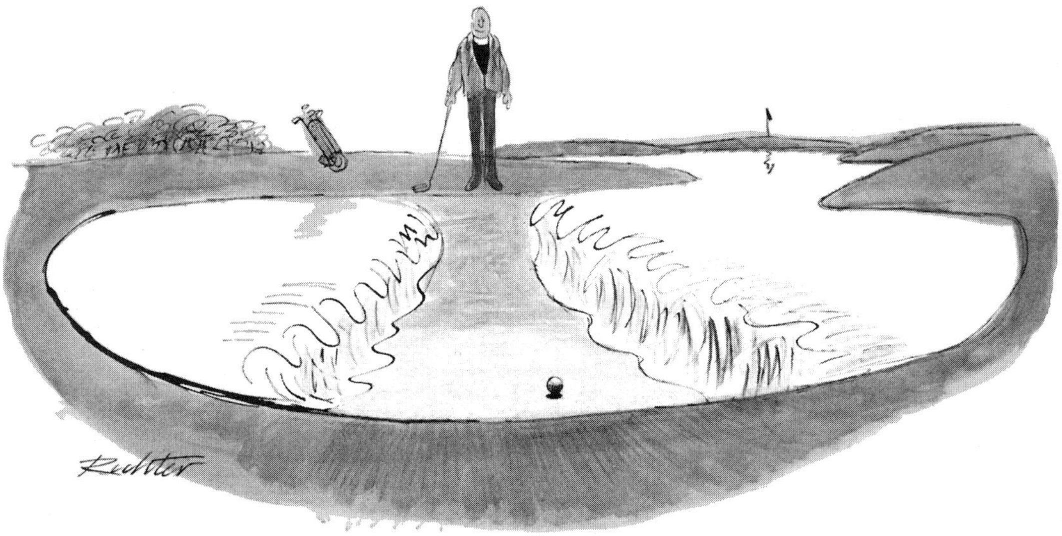
Richter

"No matter __how__ I treated you, Julia,
haunting a man at golf is hitting below the belt."

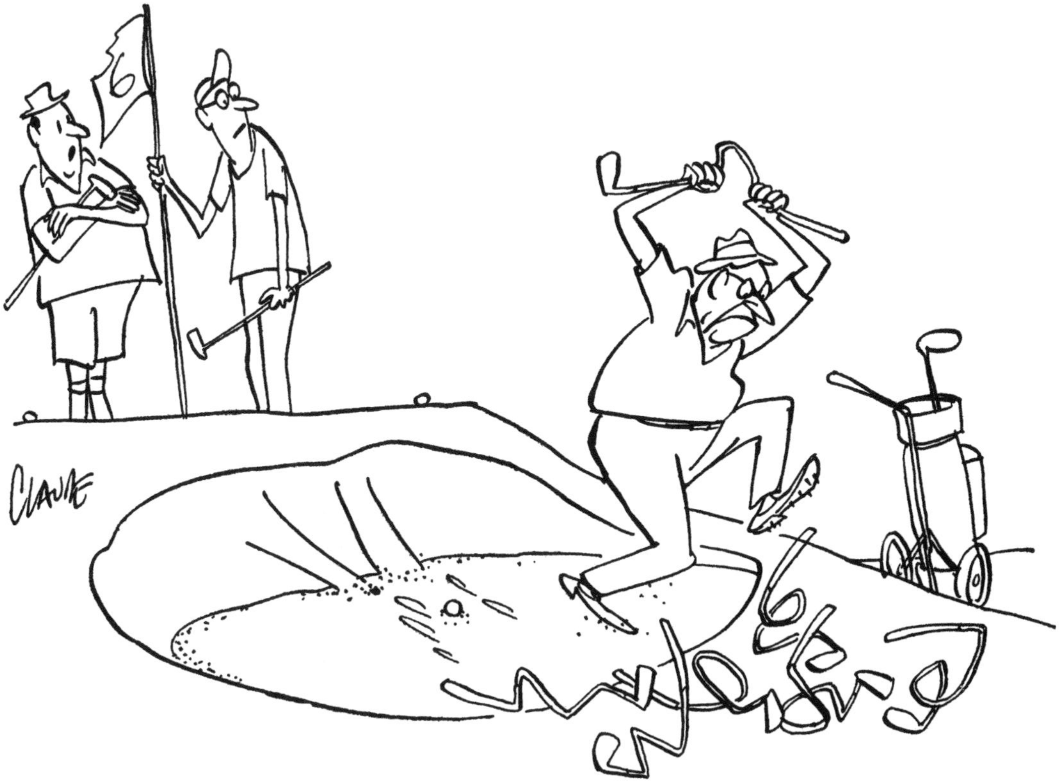

CLAUDE

"For a man of his years, he's certainly kept in marvellous condition!"

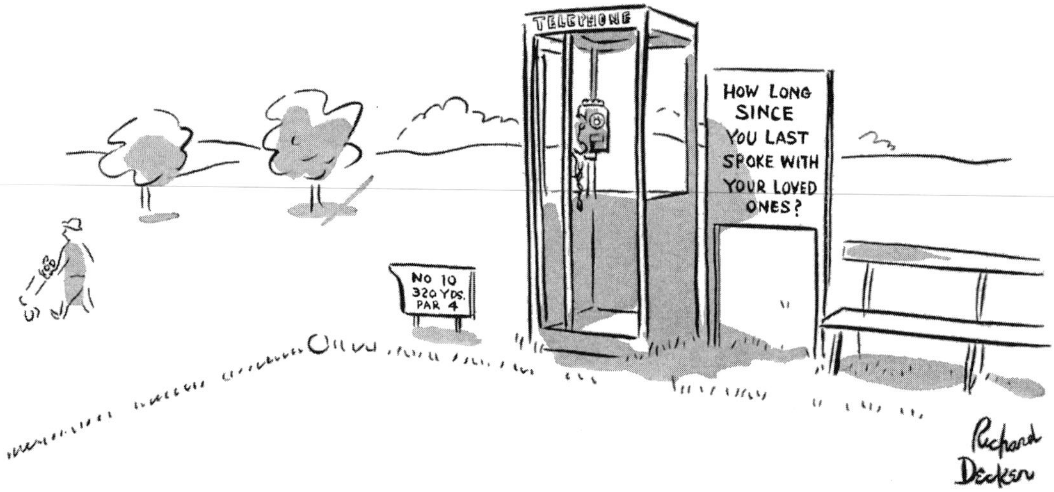
TELEPHONE
HOW LONG SINCE YOU LAST SPOKE WITH YOUR LOVED ONES?
NO 10
320 YDS.
PAR 4
Richard Decker

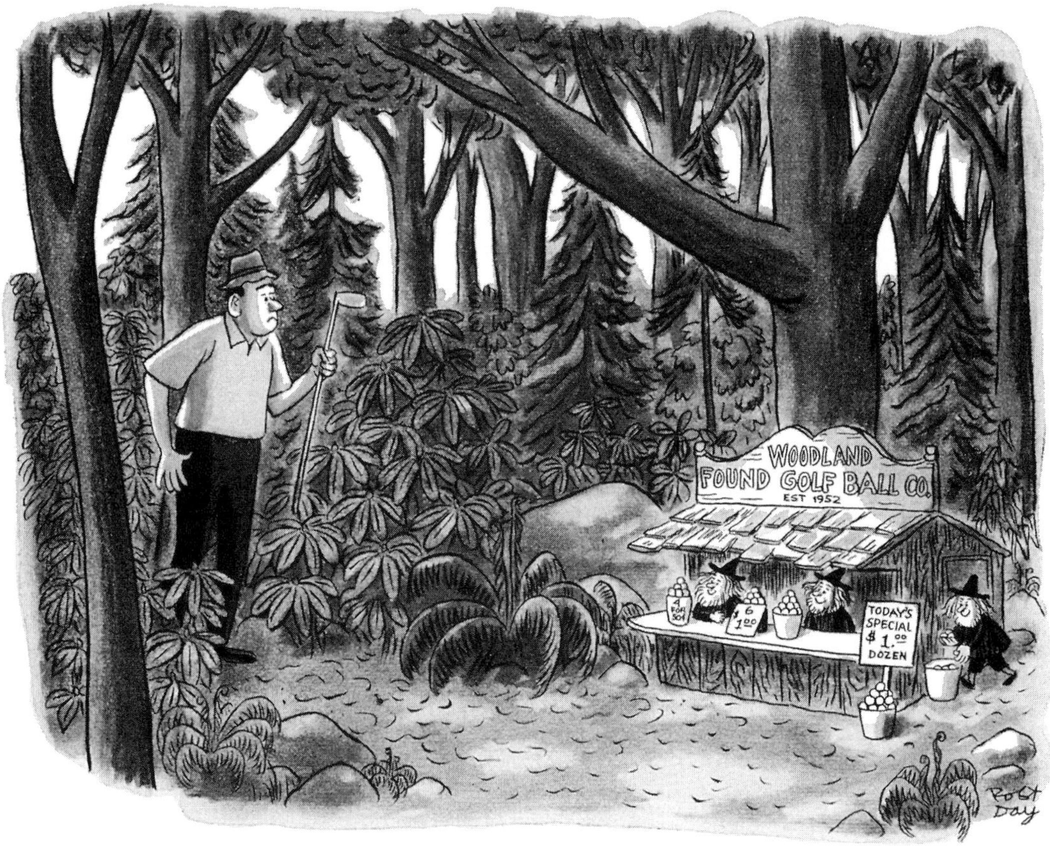
WOODLAND
FOUND GOLF BALL CO.
EST 1952
TODAY'S SPECIAL $1.00 DOZEN
Robt Day

4
5
6
PBarlow

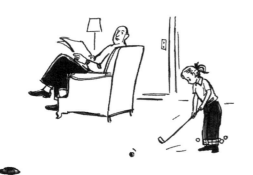

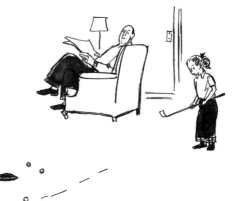

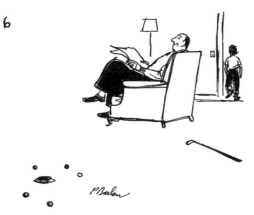

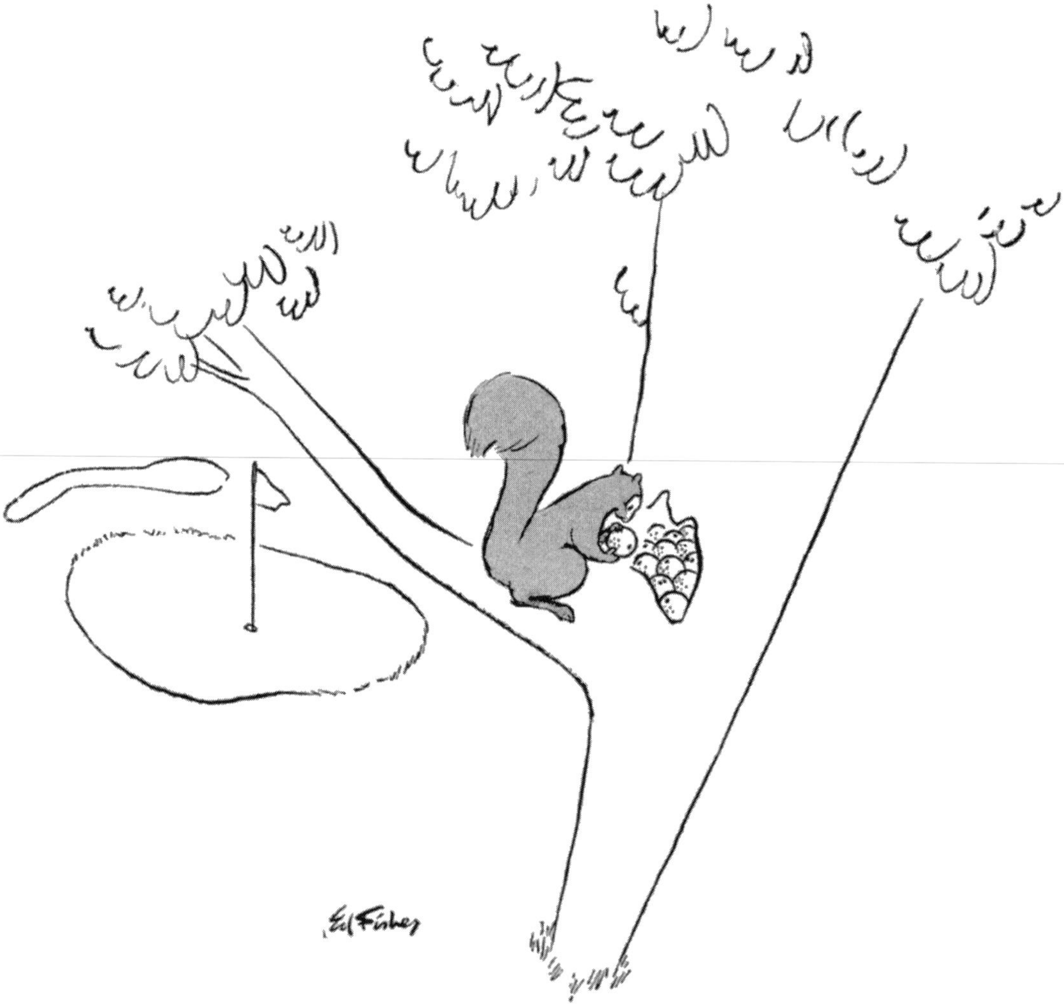
Ed Fisher

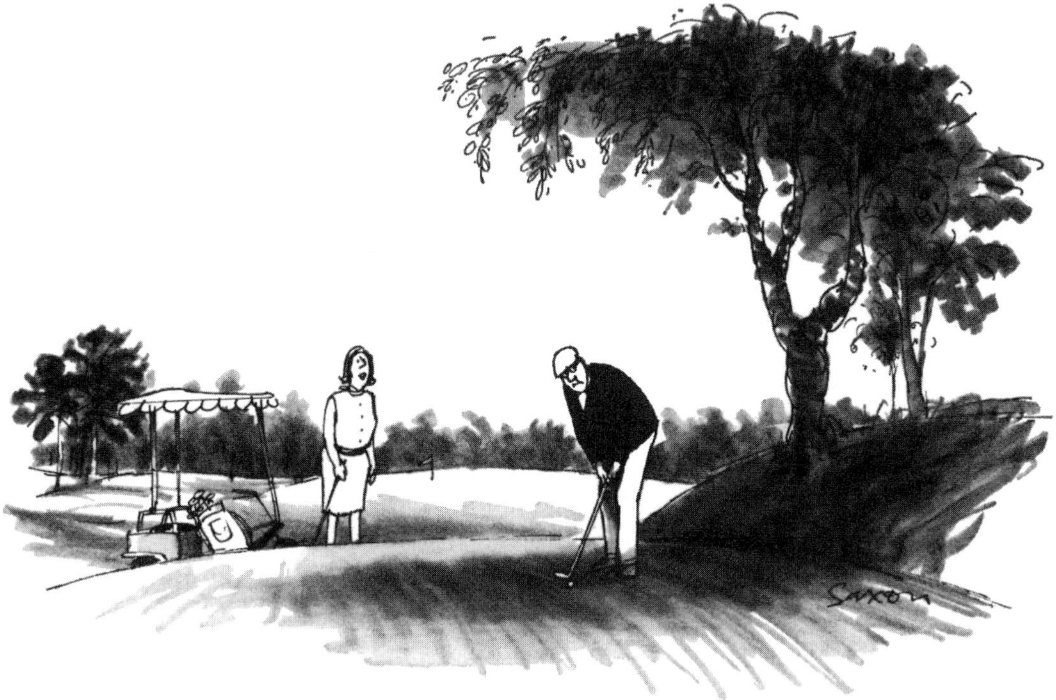
Saxon

"First you must be at peace with yourself. Then you can be at peace with the ball."

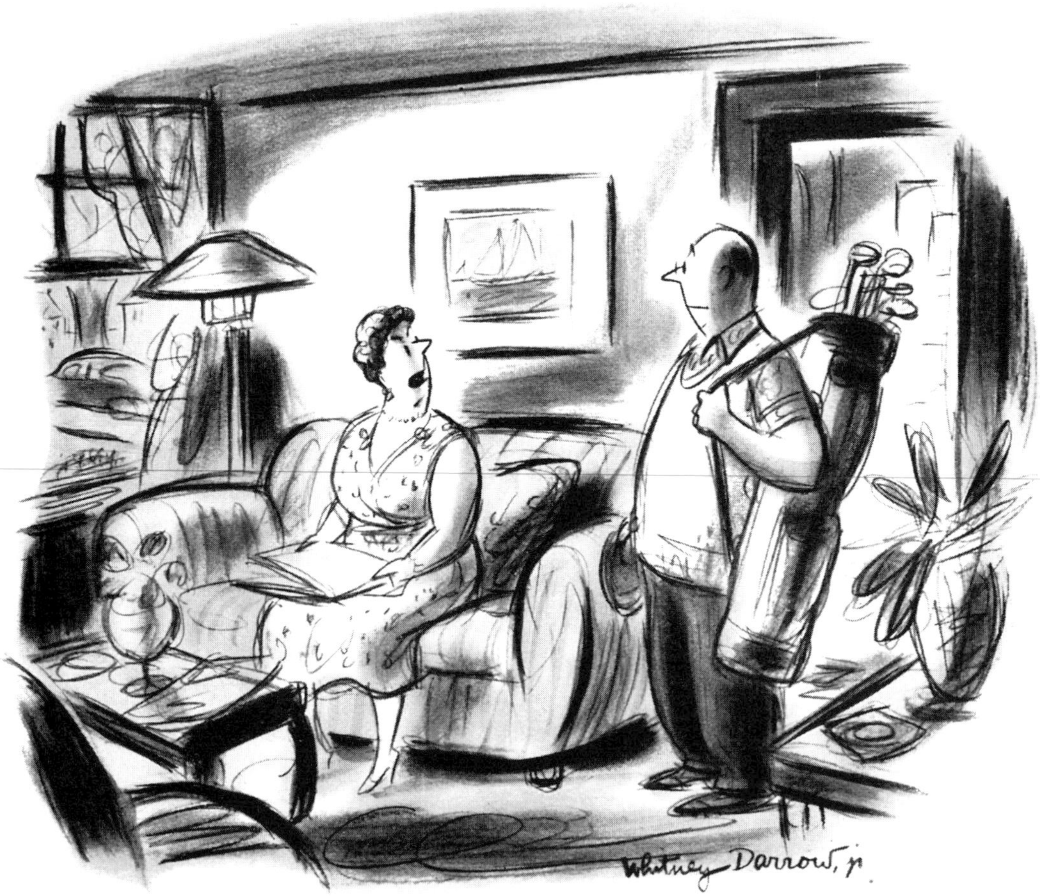
Whitney Darrow, jr.

"Well, if you broke eighty, why didn't you get home earlier?"

"Is that what they teach you at caddy school, boy? How to stare at people?"

START

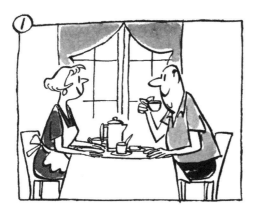

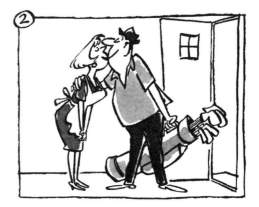

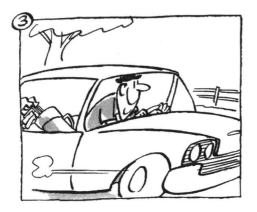

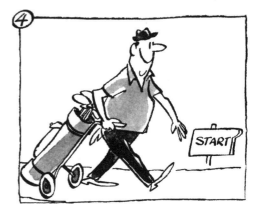

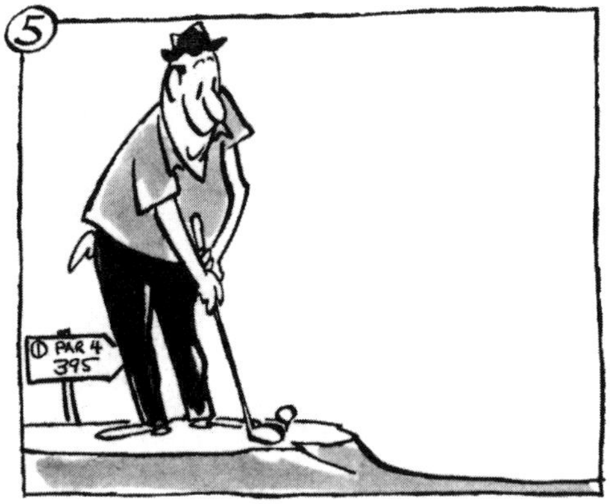
5
① PAR 4
395

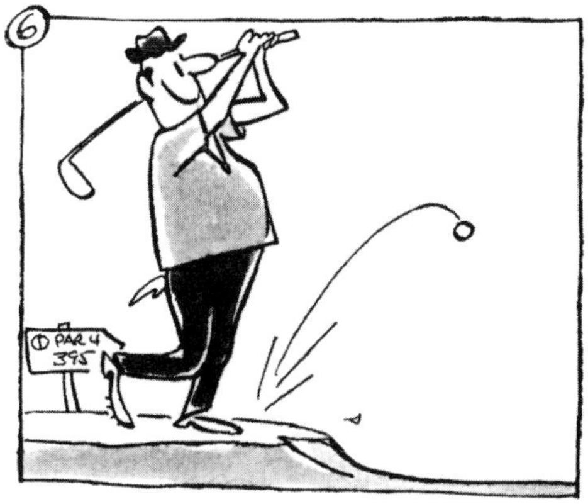
6
① PAR 4
395

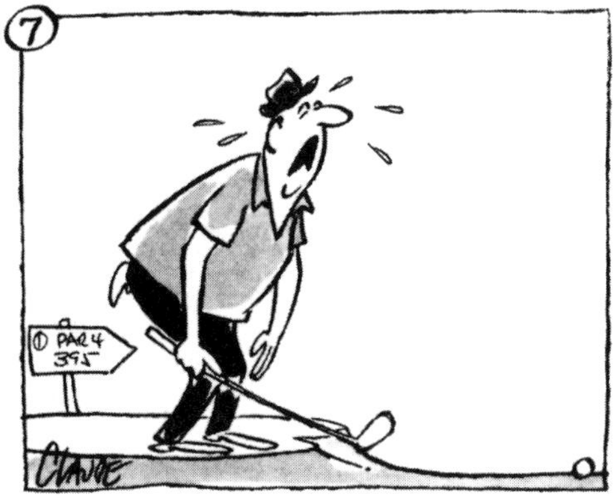
7
① PAR 4
395

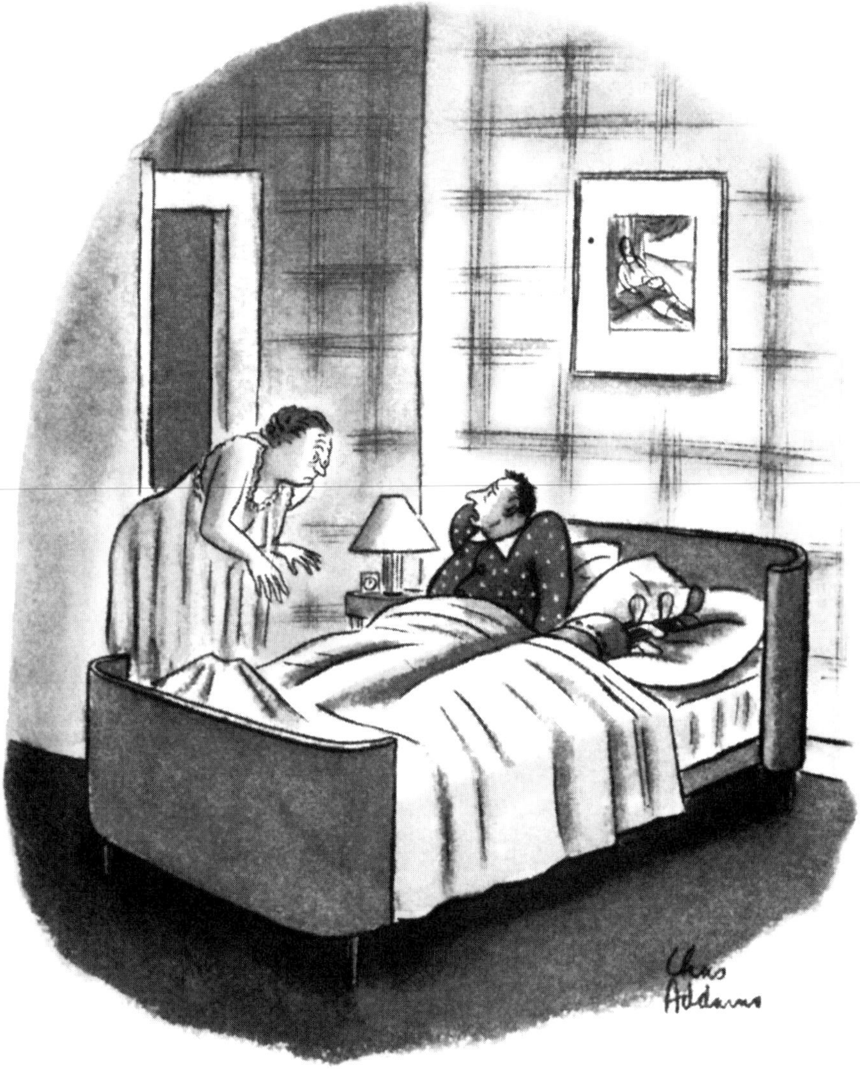
Chas Addams

"Well, you said I had to choose, didn't you?"

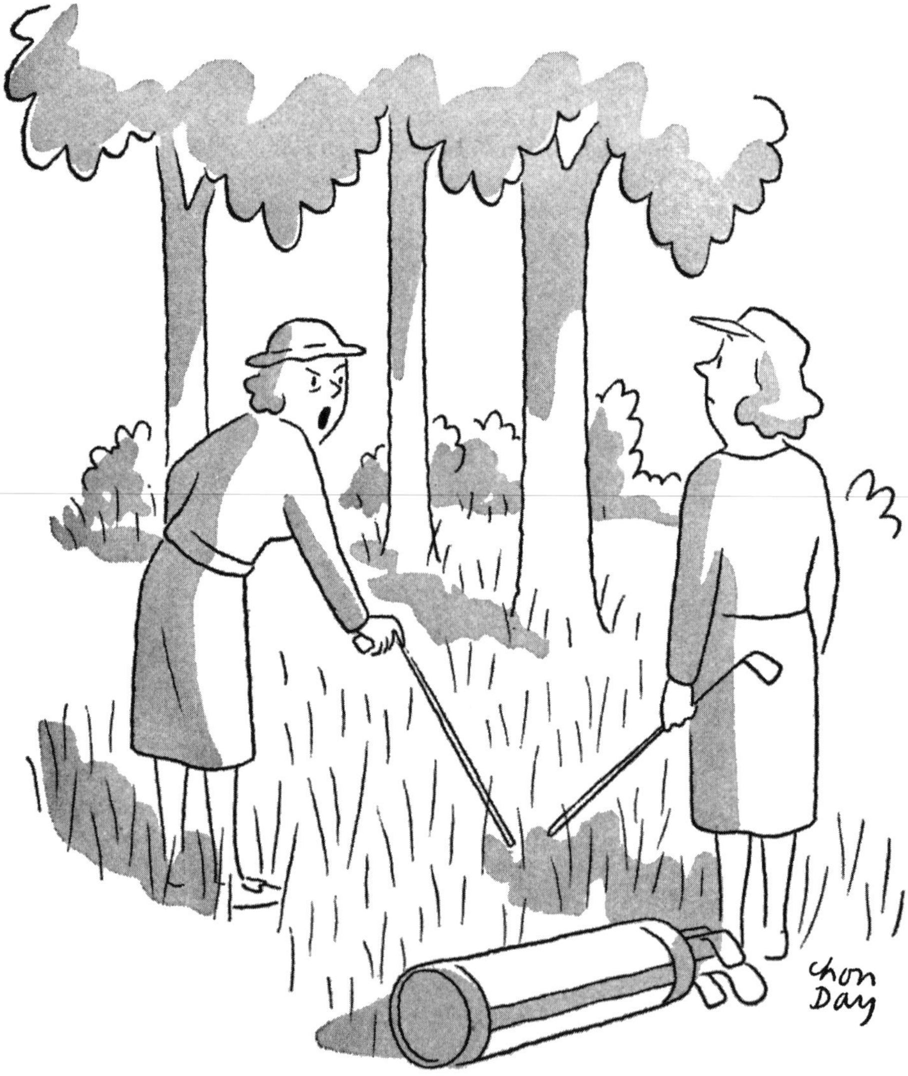
Chon Day

"I hate par."

"I'm terribly sorry. It's that confounded hook again."

"*Well, if it isn't Ed Grady! What are you doing in this neck of the woods?*"

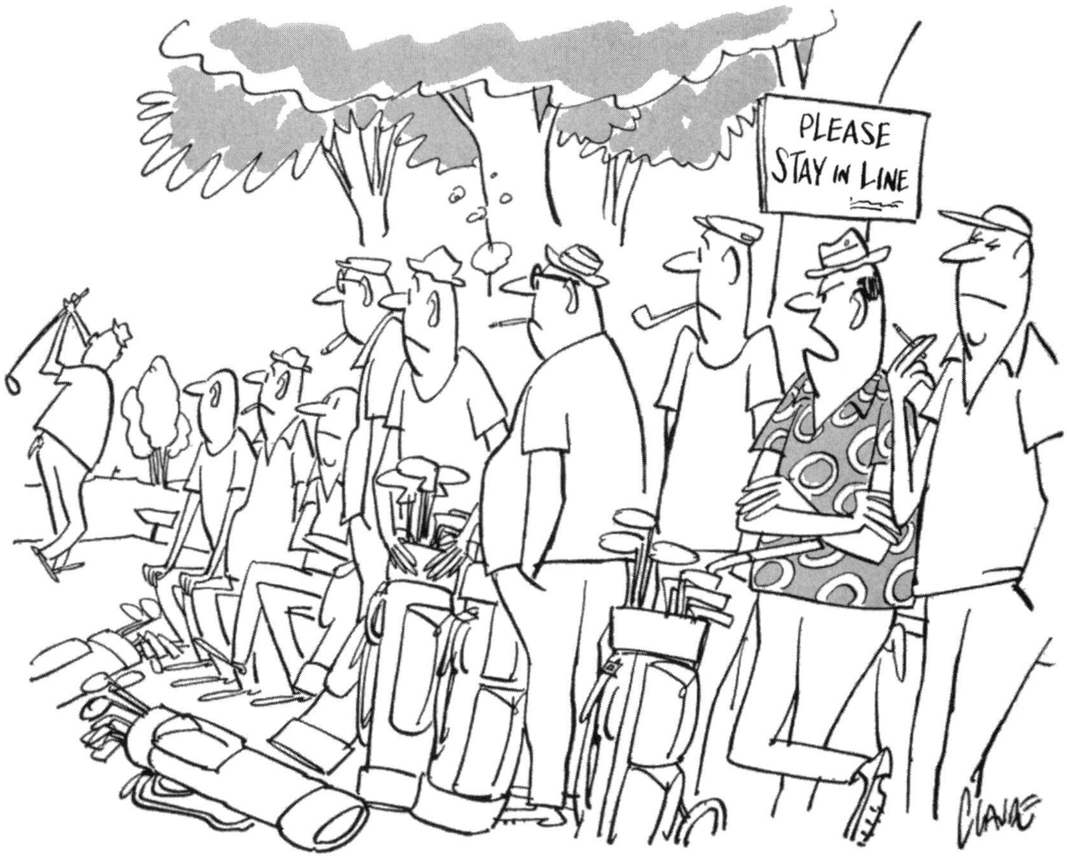
PLEASE
STAY IN LINE

"Business must really be on the skids. This is the longest we've ever had to wait on a weekday."

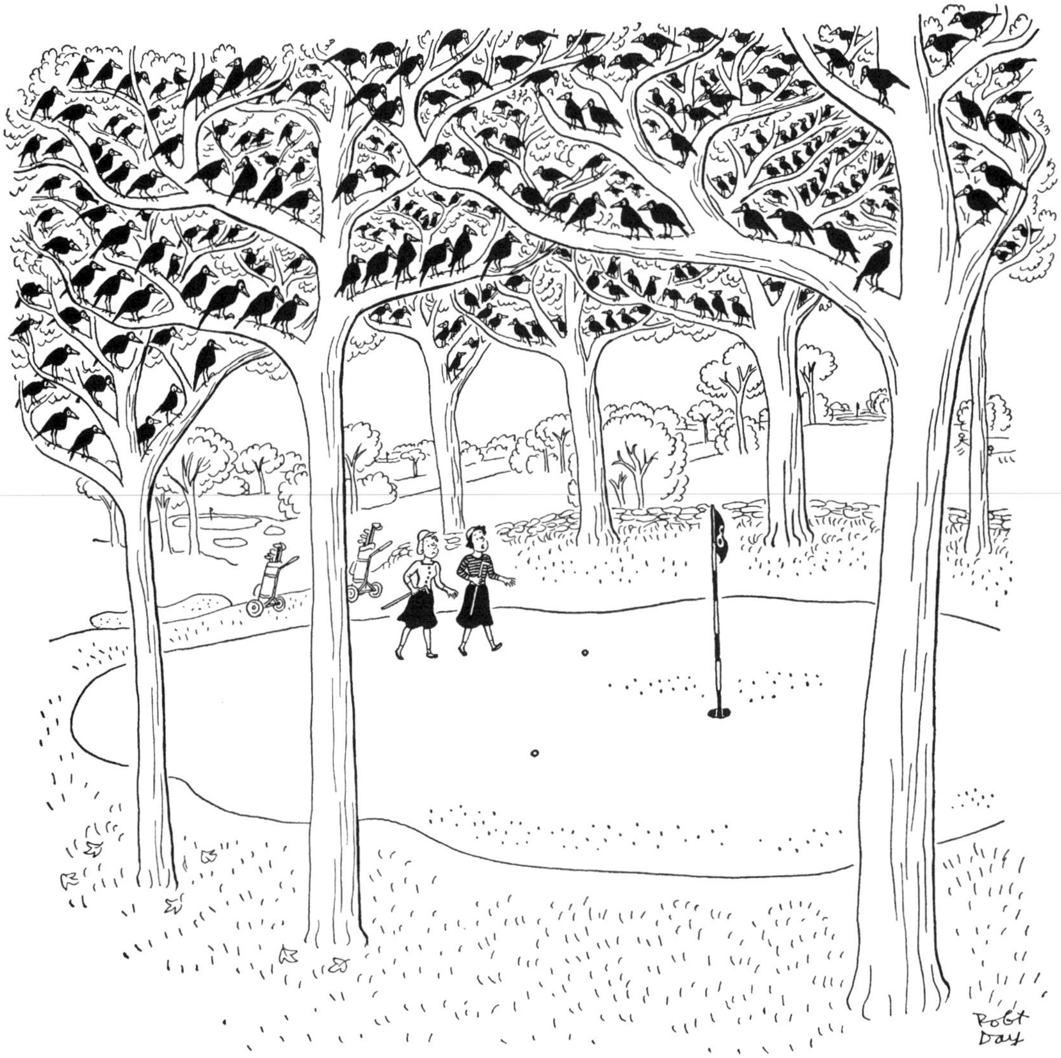
Robt Day

"I've been through this before. Flub one and their caws are deafening."

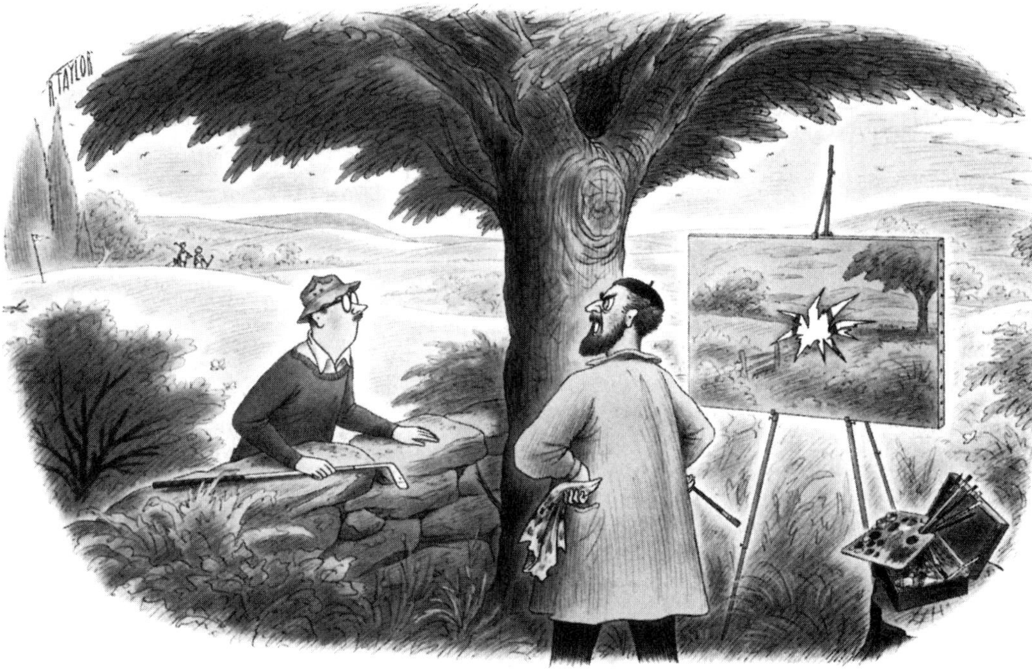
R. TAYLOR

"Yes, I have seen your ball."

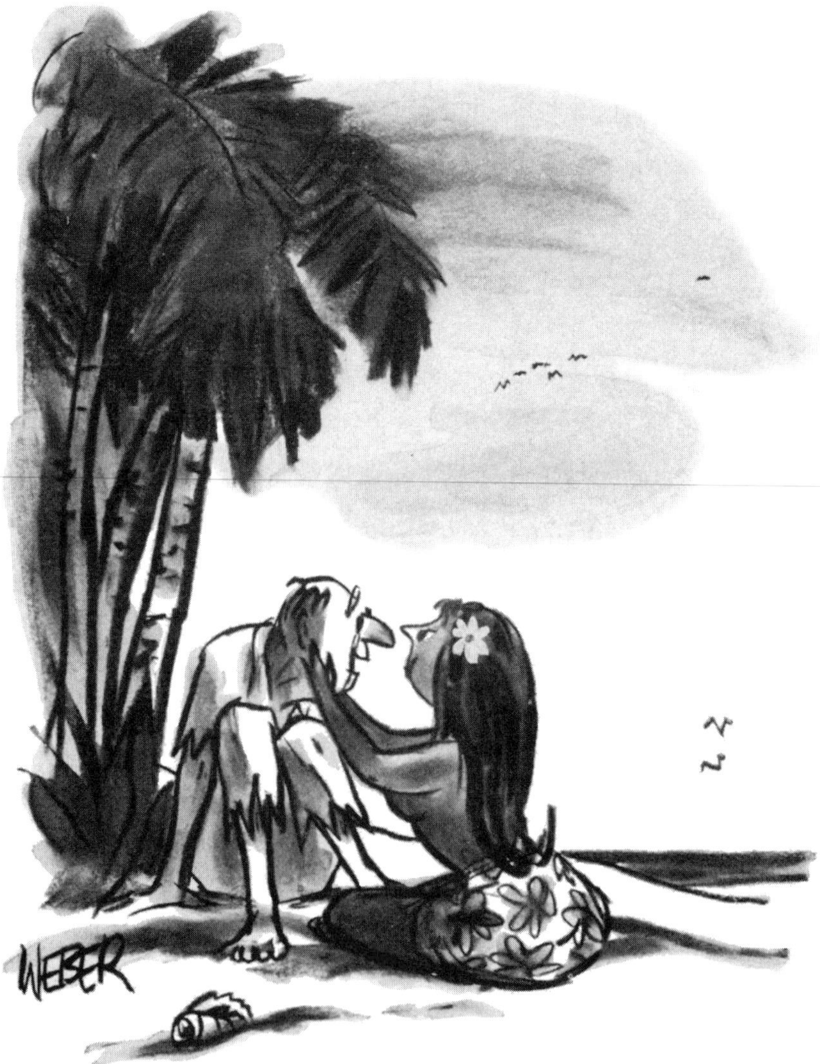
WEBER

"By George, do you know what I'm going to do? I'm going to teach you how to play golf!"

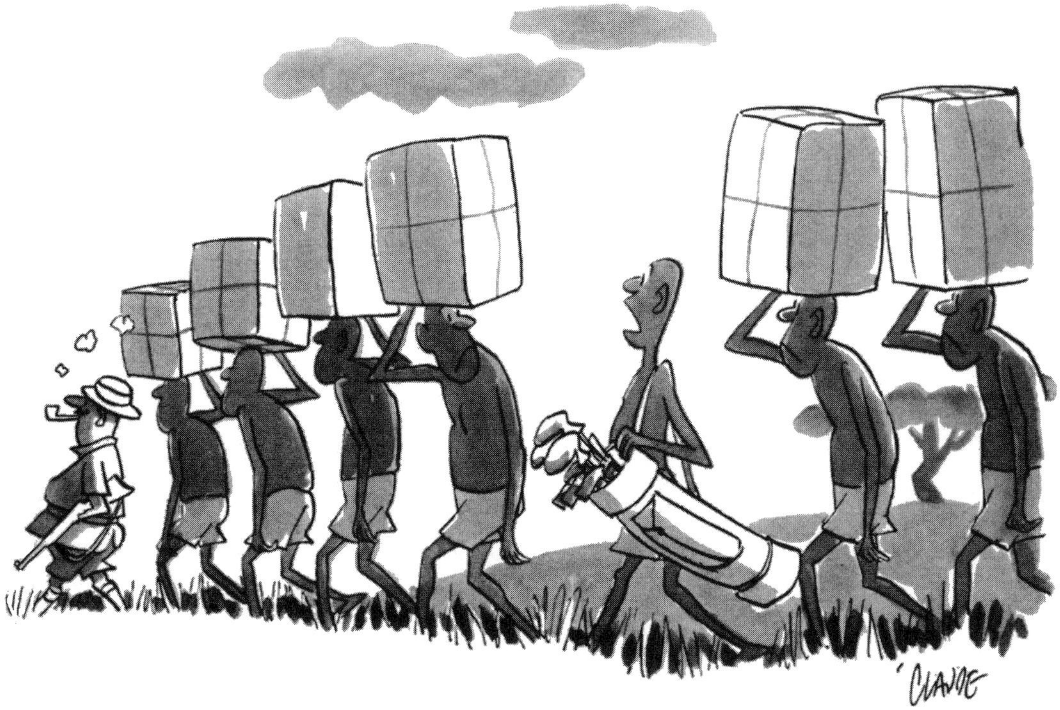
CLAUDE

"I feel like a damn fool."

"Let's not spoil it by keeping score."

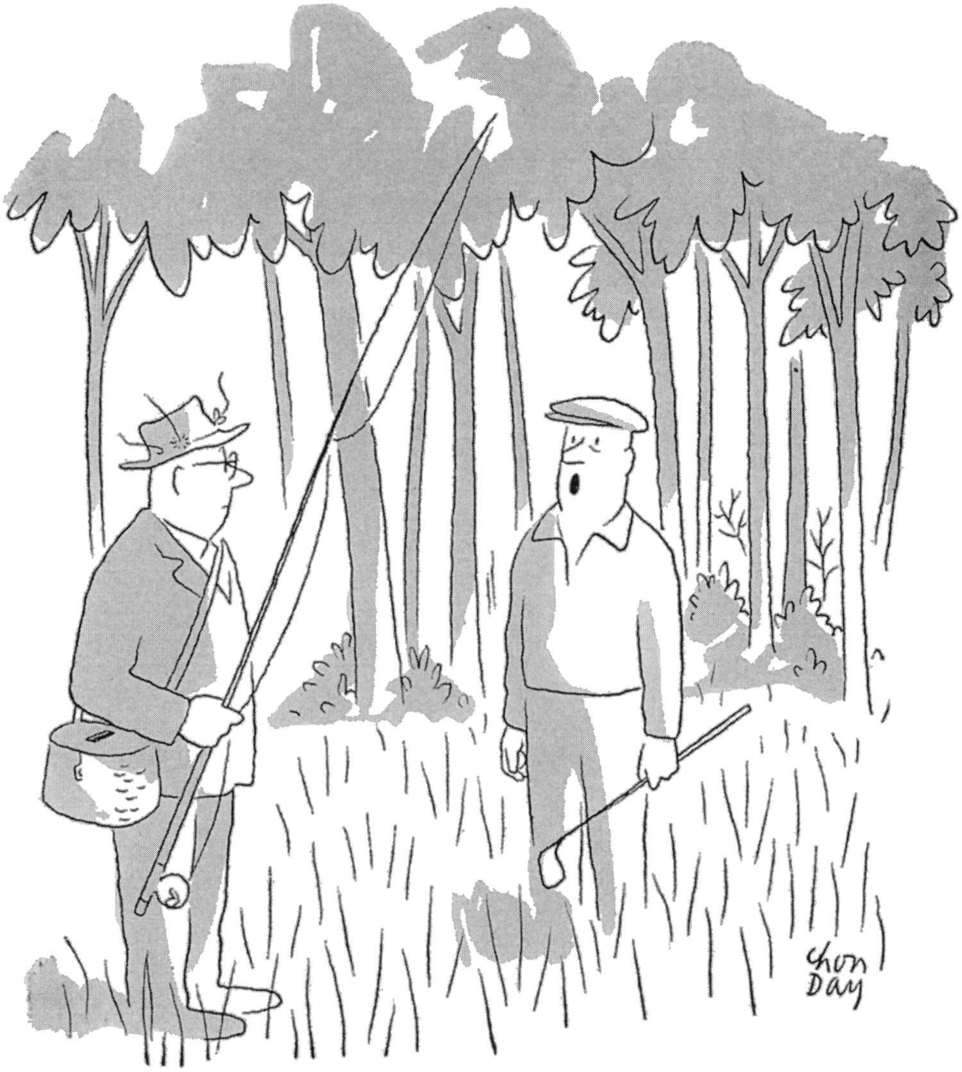
Chon Day

"No, I found my ball. I'm looking for the golf course."

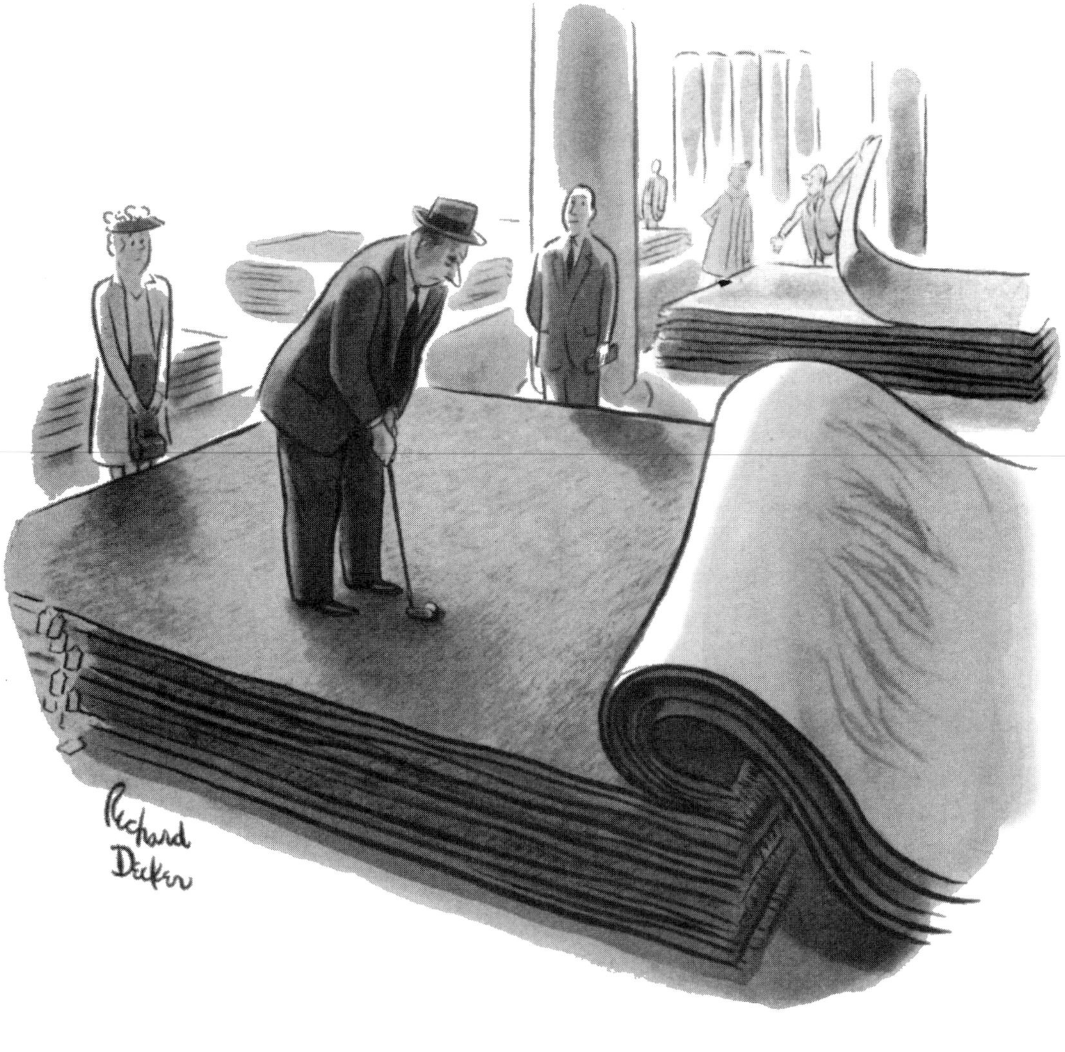
Richard Decker

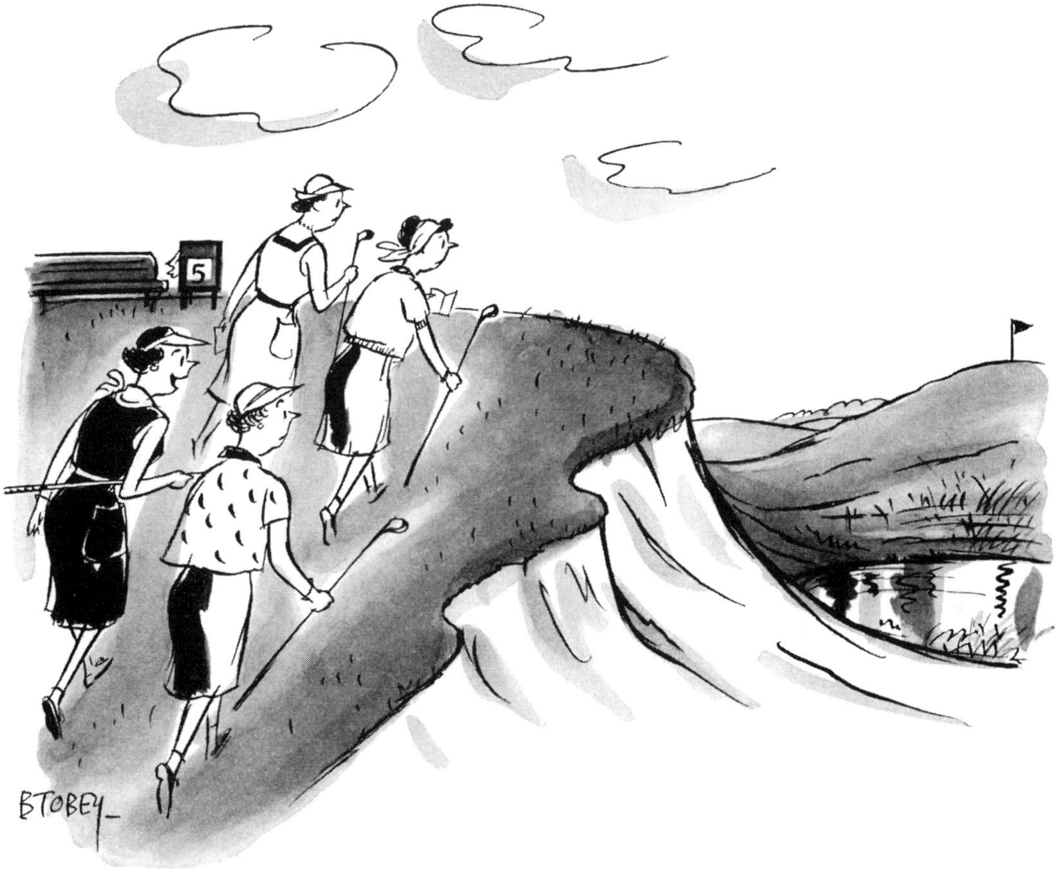
5
B TOBEY

"This is the hole that separates the women from the girls."

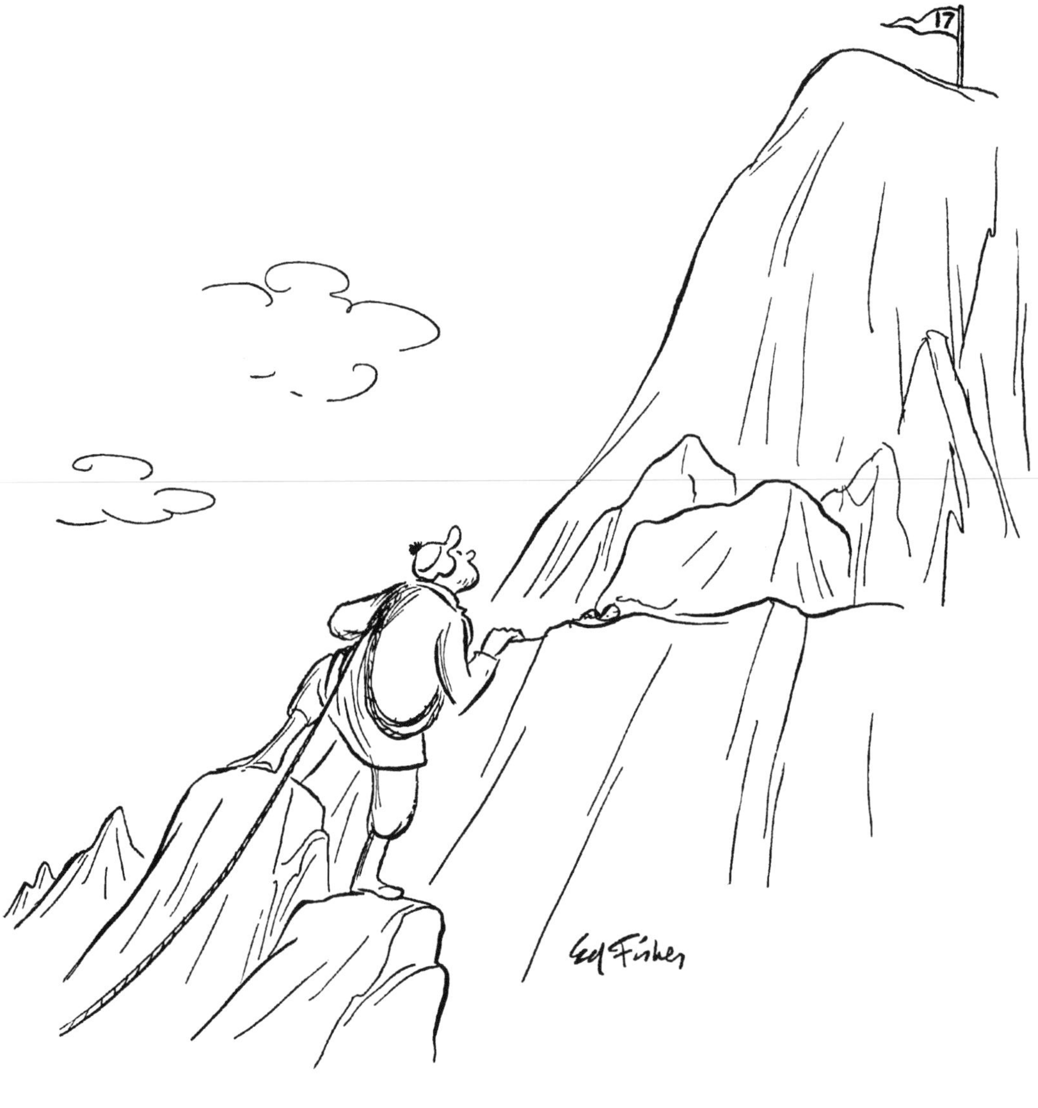

17
Ed Fisher

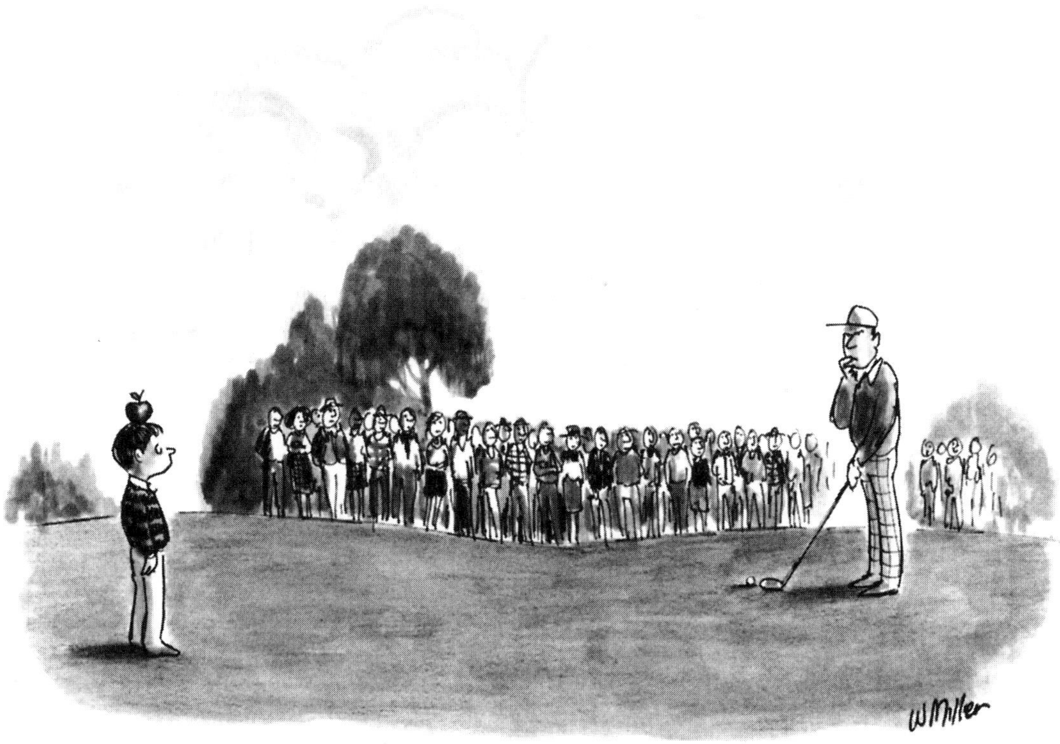
W Miller

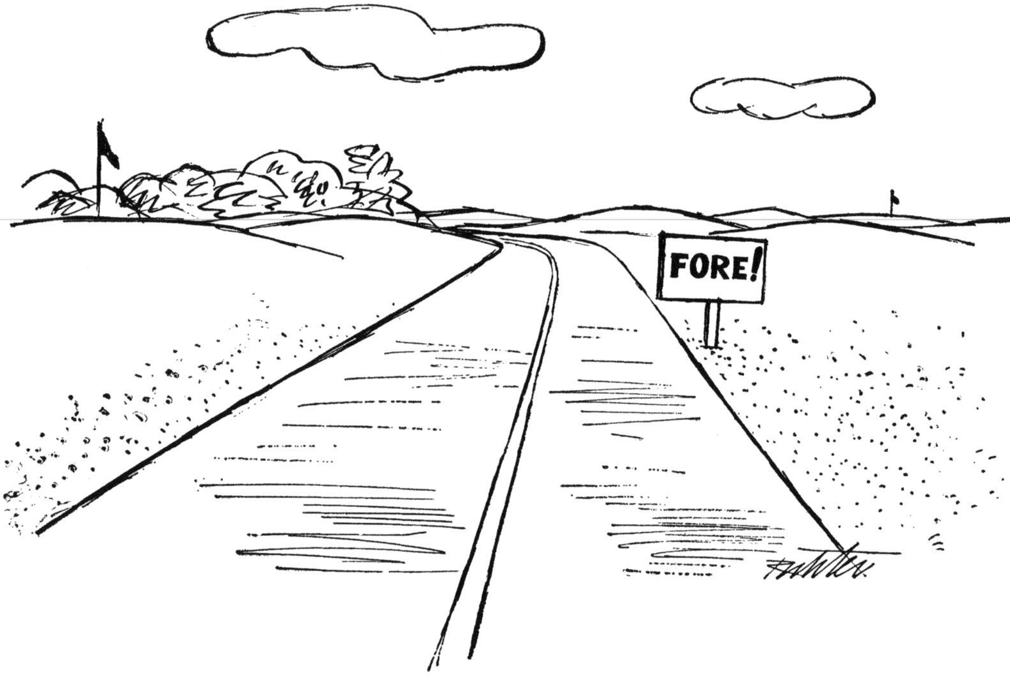
FORE!

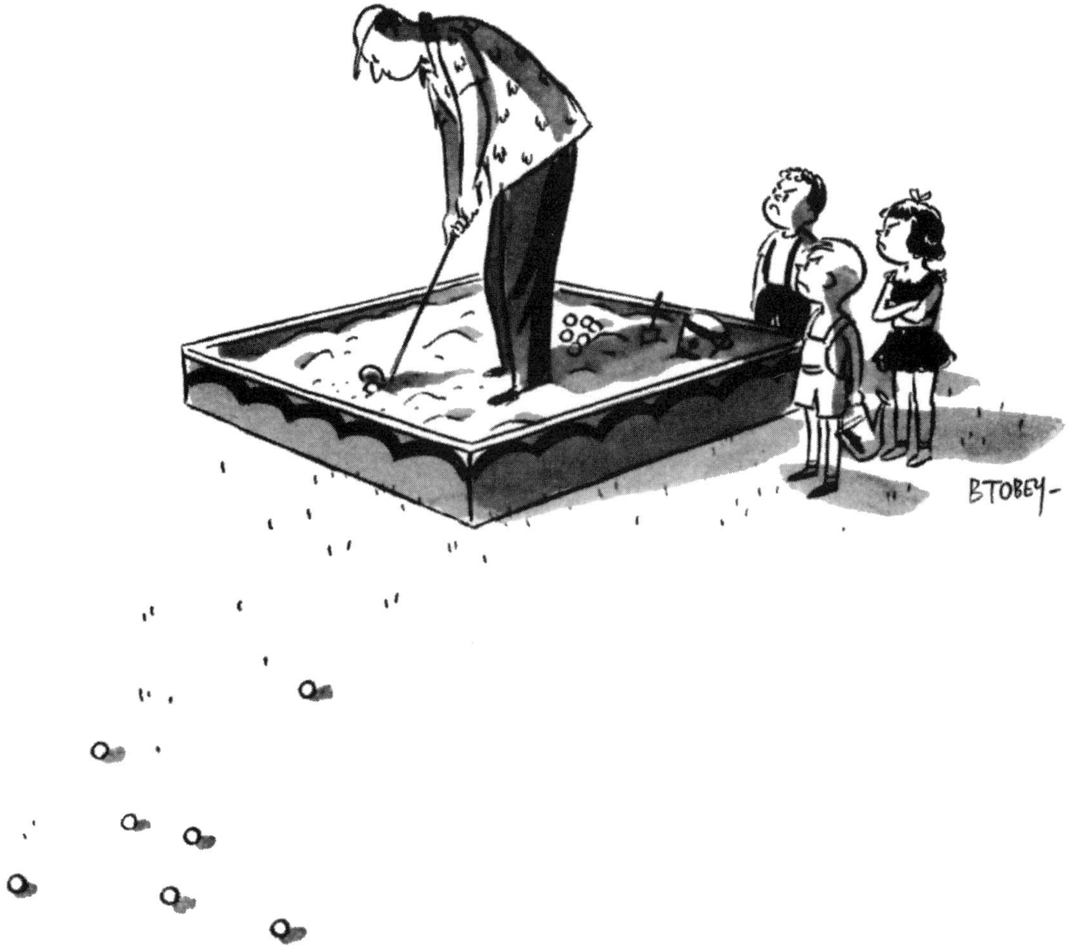
B TOBEY

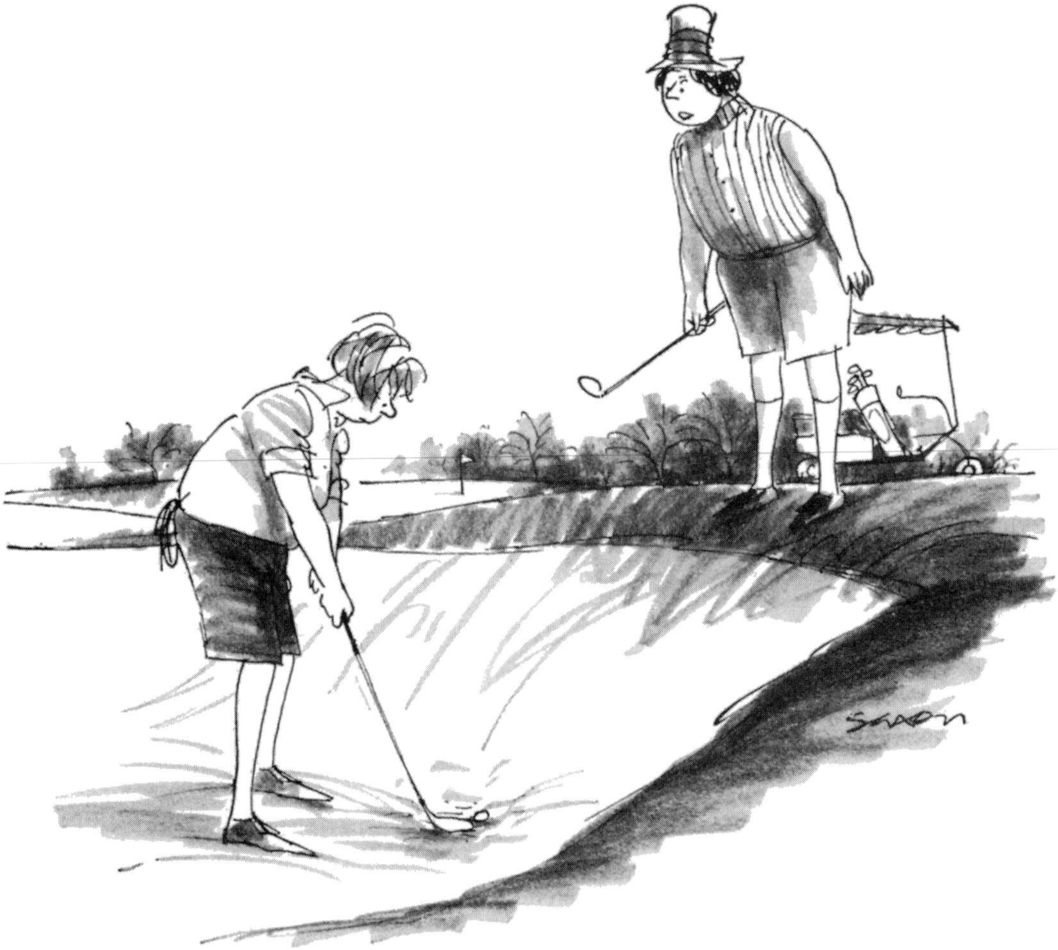
Saxon

"Think beautiful thoughts."

"Never ask what kind of a round
they had. If they want you to know, they'll tell you."

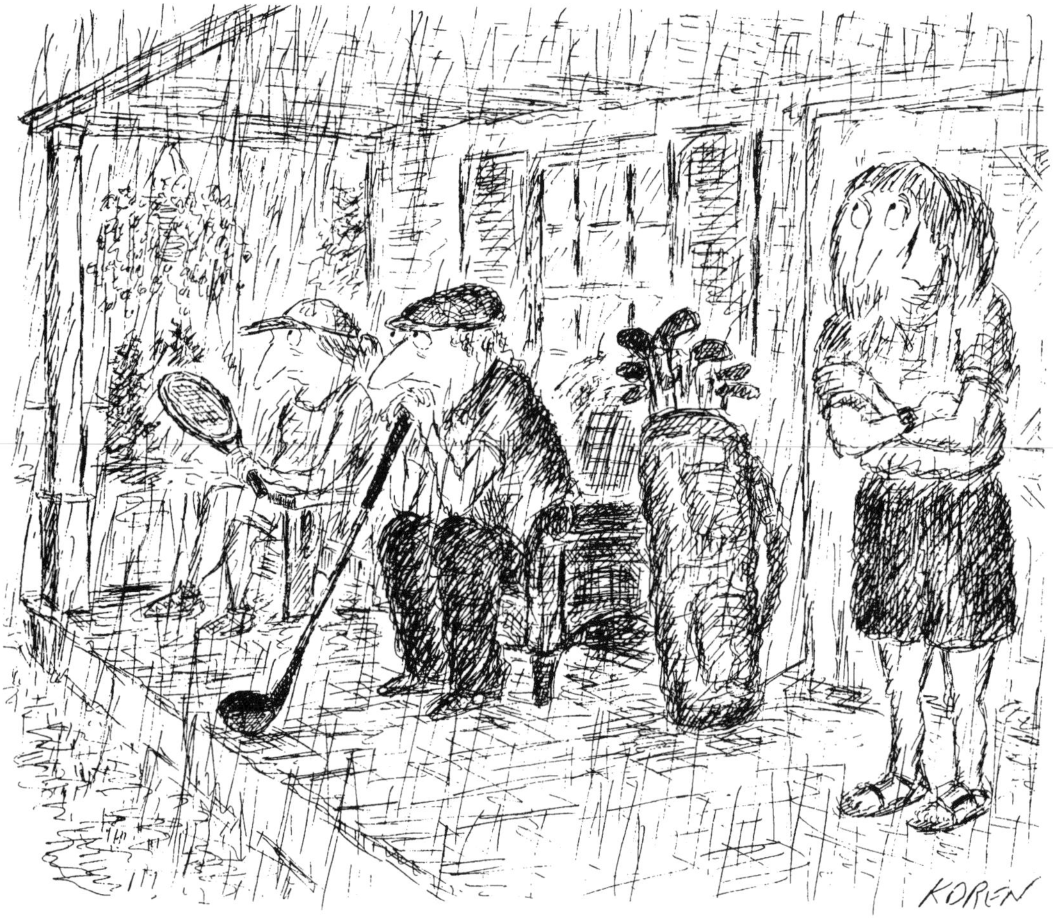
KOREN

"Well, it has been a great summer for chanterelles."

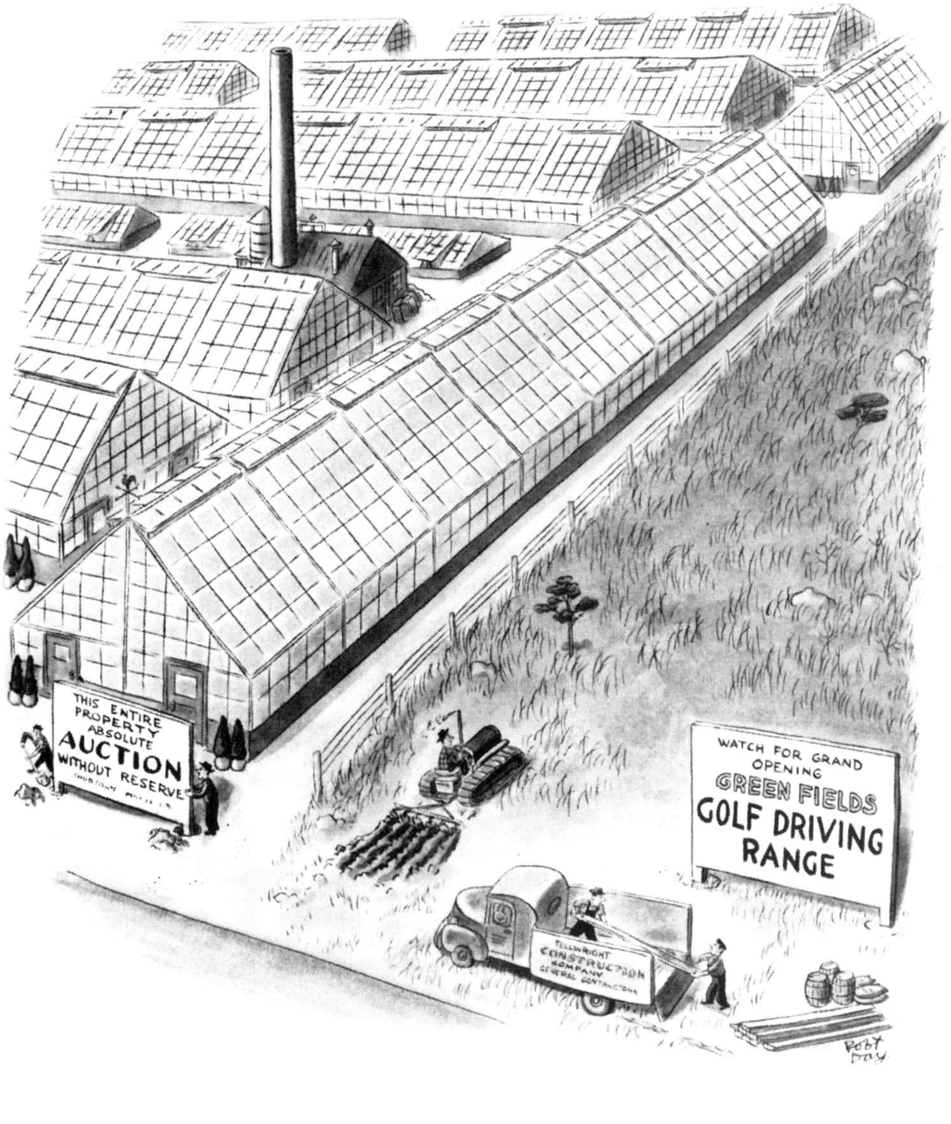
THIS ENTIRE PROPERTY ABSOLUTE
AUCTION
WITHOUT RESERVE
WATCH FOR GRAND OPENING
GREEN FIELDS
GOLF DRIVING RANGE
CONSTRUCTION COMPANY
GENERAL CONTRACTORS

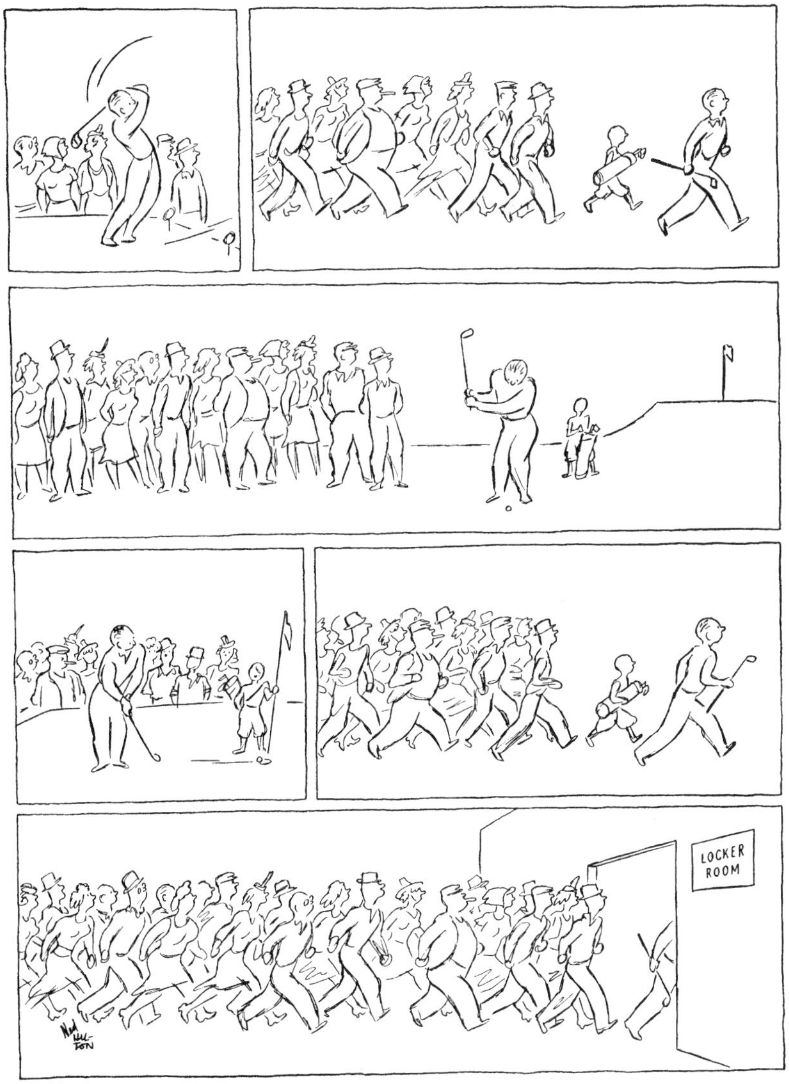
LOCKER ROOM

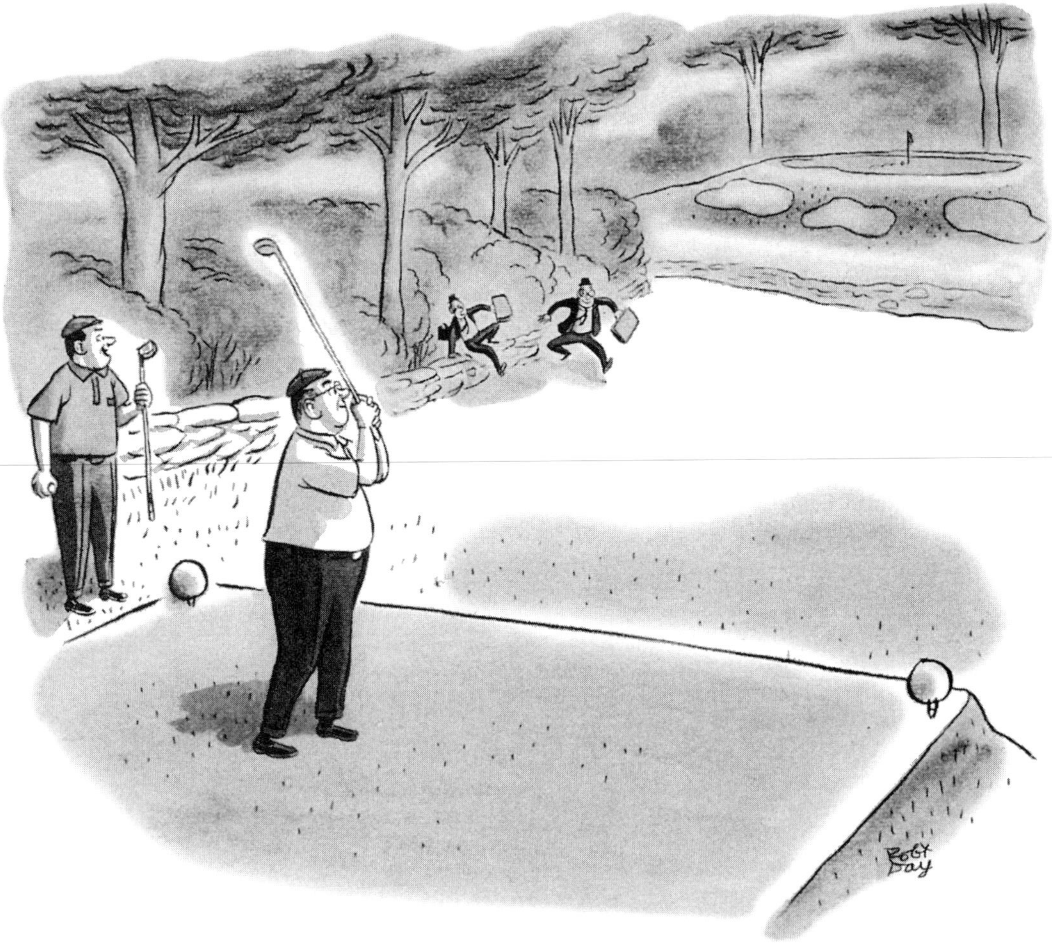
Robt Day

"I had a hunch you might be agreeable to that merger idea, so I arranged for our legal chaps to be on hand just in case."

"Have a good day, now, and break whatever it is you're supposed to break."

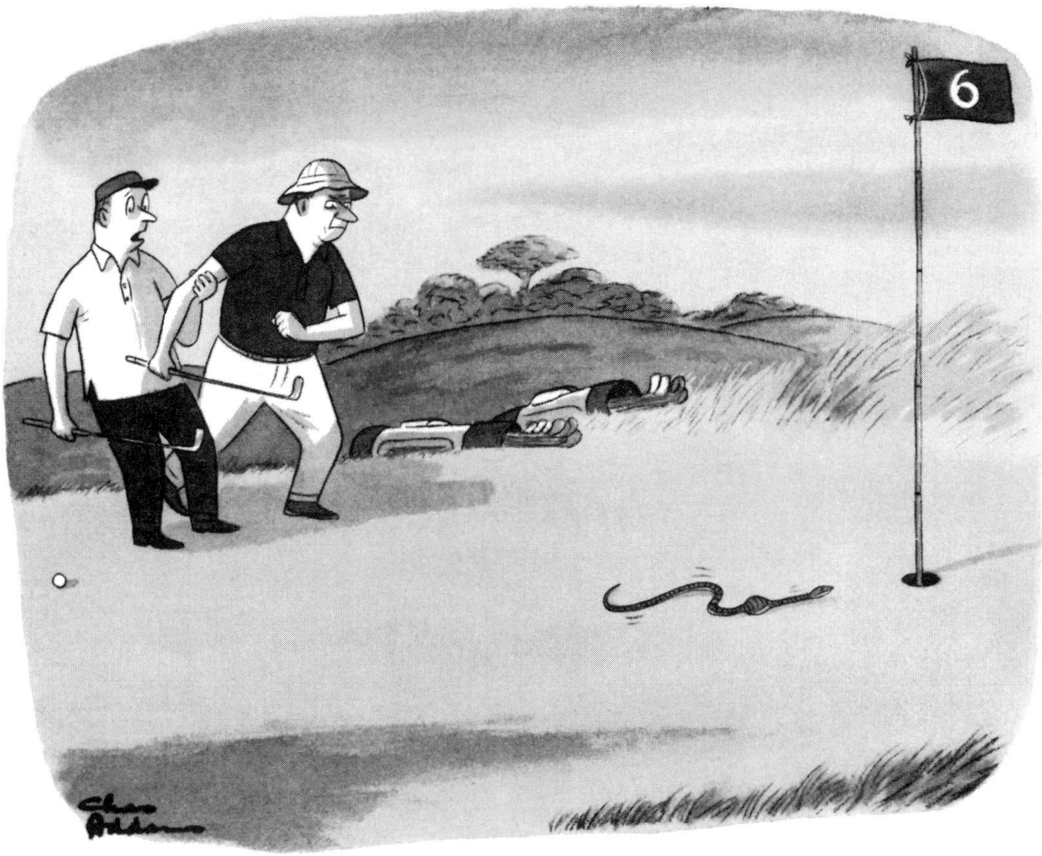
6
Chas Addams

"Take it easy. You may get your birdie yet."

1

2

3

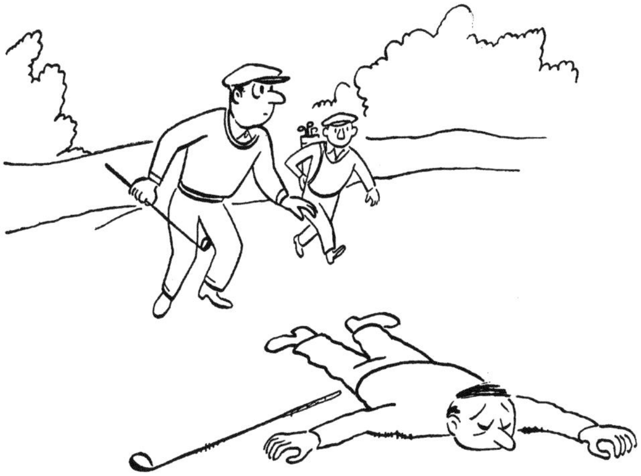

4

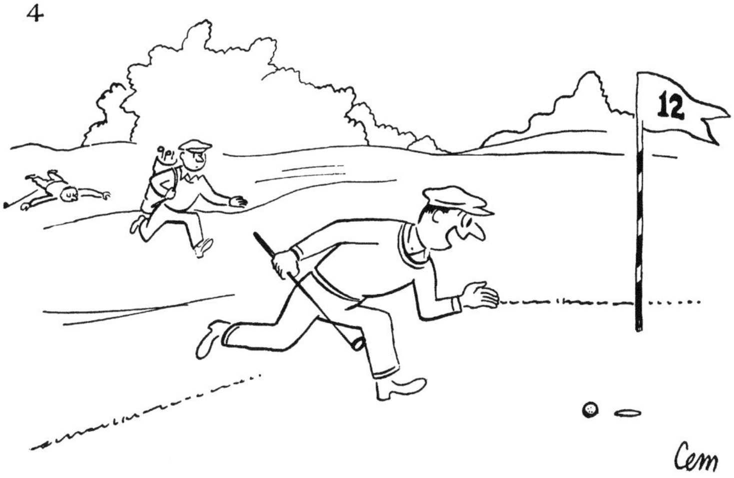
12
Cem

HOLE IN FORTY-SEVEN

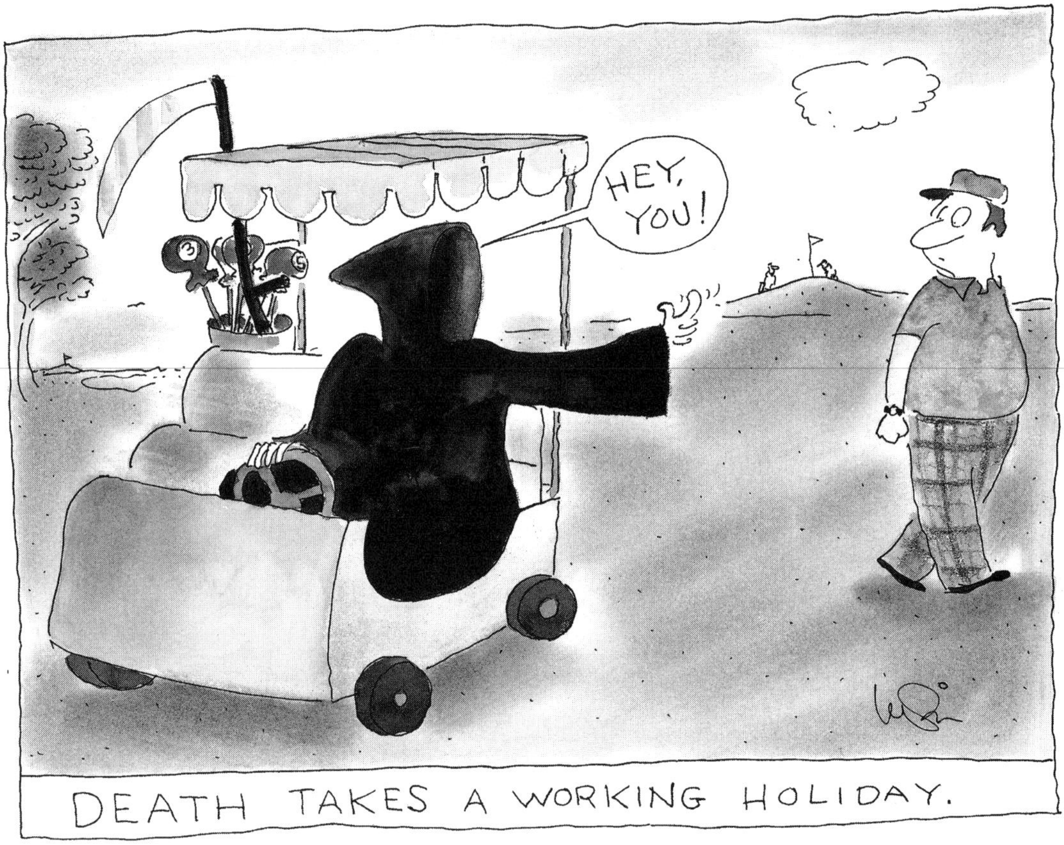
HEY, YOU!

DEATH TAKES A WORKING HOLIDAY.

INDEX OF ARTISTS